Top Tips from the Baby Whisperer for Toddlers

Top Tips from the Baby Whisperer for Toddlers

Secrets to Raising Happy
and Cooperative Toddlers

Tracy Hogg
with Melinda Blau

1 3 5 7 9 10 8 6 4 2

Published in 2008 by Vermilion, an imprint of Ebury Publishing

Ebury Publishing is a Random House Group company

Copyright © Tracy Hogg Enterprises, Inc. 2001

Tracy Hogg has asserted her right to be identified as the author of this Work
in accordance with the Copyright, Designs and Patents Act 1988

All rights reserved. No part of this publication may be reproduced, stored in a
retrieval system, or transmitted in any form or by any means, electronic, mechanical,
photocopying, recording or otherwise, without the prior permission of the copyright owner

The Random House Group Limited Reg. No. 954009

Addresses for companies within the Random House Group can be found at

www.rbooks.co.uk

A CIP catalogue record for this book is available from the British Library

Mixed Sources
Product group from well-managed
forests and other controlled sources
www.fsc.org Cert no. TT-COC-2139
© 1996 Forest Stewardship Council

The Random House Group Limited supports The Forest Stewardship Council (FSC),
the leading international forest certification organisation. All our titles that are printed on
Greenpeace approved FSC certified paper carry the FSC logo. Our paper procurement policy
can be found at www.rbooks.co.uk/environment

Typeset by SX DTP, Rayleigh, Essex

Printed and bound in the UK by CPI Mackays, Chatham ME5 8TD

ISBN 978 0 09 191743 2

Copies are available at special rates for bulk orders. Contact the sales
development team on 020 7840 8487 for more information.

To buy books by your favourite authors and register for offers, visit www.rbooks.co.uk

Contents

Introduction

The Challenge of Toddlerhood

Welcome to what is probably the most strenuous and awe-inspiring stage of parenting.

The dictionary defines a toddler as 'a small child roughly between the ages of one and three'. Other books mark this phase of childhood when a baby first begins to 'toddle', or walk with short, unsteady steps. For some, this can be as young as eight or nine months. Either way, trust me, if you have a toddler on your hands, you know it, no matter what a book tells you.

Baby Whispering: The Foundation of Good Parenting

Having cared for over 5,000 babies, I fine-tuned what one of my clients dubbed 'baby whispering'. It's quite like what a horse whisperer does, but here we're talking about infants. In both cases, we're dealing with sensate creatures, living beings who can't actually talk but express themselves nevertheless. In order to care for and connect with them, we must learn their language. Hence, baby whispering means tuning in, observing, listening and understanding what's happening from the child's perspective.

If you have already read *Secrets of the Baby Whisperer*, the following will be familiar. Think of it as a refresher course.

Every child is an individual

From the day a baby is born, she has a unique personality, as well as likes and dislikes of her own. Therefore no one strategy works for all. You have to find out what's right for your toddler.

Every child deserves respect – and must learn to respect others as well

We need to draw what I call a circle of respect around each child – an invisible boundary beyond which we don't go without asking permission or explaining what we're about to do.

Children at this age can be rather demanding and obstinate, and they have to learn to respect us as well. In these pages, I'll teach you how to respect your toddler and meet her needs without compromising your own boundaries.

Take the time to observe, listen and talk with children, not at them

The process of getting to know your child starts the day he comes into the world. By observing, we begin to understand a toddler's unique temperament. By listening to him, even before he acquires spoken language, we begin to know what he wants. And by having a dialogue – conversing rather than lecturing – we allow the child to express who he really is.

Every child needs a structured routine, which gives her life predictability and safety

As parents and caretakers, we provide consistency and safety through ritual, routines and rules. It's a paradox of sorts, allowing a child to explore and simultaneously making sure she knows that she has to live within the safe confines we create for her.

The above simple, down-to-earth guidelines provide the foundation upon which a solid family is built. Children thrive when they are listened to, understood and treated with respect. They thrive when they know what's expected of them and what they can expect of the world around them.

My Intentions: The Road to Harmony

I've outlined below a list of more specific goals which will encourage, teach, and demonstrate through example, how to:

- *View – and respect – your toddler as an individual.* Rather than categorising him by age, allow him to be who he is.

- *Cheer your toddler on towards independence – without rushing him.* To that end, I provide tools that will help you gauge her readiness and teach her practical skills, such as eating, dressing, potty-training and basic hygiene.

- *Learn how to tune in to your child's verbal and nonverbal language.* You must exercise patience and restraint when your child is trying to tell you something and, at the same time, know when to step in and offer your help.

- *Be realistic – toddlerhood is a time of constant change.* One of the biggest challenges of parenting a toddler is that just when you get used to a certain kind of behaviour or a particular level of competence – bam! – your child changes.

- *Promote your child's development and family harmony.* It's critical to create a happy, safe environment that enables a child to venture forth, and, at the same time, keeps him out of harm's way and doesn't allow his antics to disrupt the family.

- *Help your toddler manage her emotions – particularly her frustrations.* Studies have shown that children as young as 14 months can begin to identify and even anticipate mood (theirs and their caretakers'), feel empathy and, as soon as they're verbal, talk about feelings as well. It is important to remember that emotional skills can be learned and as your toddler's emotional repertoire expands there will be a growing awareness of herself and of social situations.

- *Develop a strong meaningful bond between Dad and your toddler.* In most families, it still takes extra effort for Dad to be more than a Saturday helper. We need to look at ways for fathers to be truly involved, connecting emotionally, not just as a play pal.

- *Facilitate your child's becoming a social being.* As your toddler marches towards the preschool years, social skills become increasingly important. Therefore, he will need to develop empathy, consideration of others and the ability to negotiate and handle conflict. These skills are best taught through example, guidance and repetition.

- *Manage your emotions.* Because dealing with a toddler is so demanding, you must learn how to be patient, how and when to praise, how to see that 'giving in' isn't loving (no matter how adorable your toddler acts), how to put your love into action (not just words) and what to do when you're angry or frustrated.

- *Nourish your own adult relationships.* Toddlerhood deprives mums of downtime. You need to learn how to spend guilt-free time away from your toddler.

CHAPTER ONE
Your Toddler

When considering the delicate balance of nature/nurture I think the bottom line is that no one knows exactly how nature and nurture work, but we do know that they work together, each influencing the other. Hence, we have to respect the child nature has given us and, at the same time, give that child whatever support he or she needs. Admittedly, this is a delicate balance, especially for parents of toddlers. But following are some important ideas to keep in mind.

You first need to understand – and accept – the child you have
The idea is to look at your toddler, love her for who she is, and tailor your own ideas and behaviour to do what is best for her.

You can help your child make the most of whoever he is
Understanding your child's temperament enables you to plan ahead.

Your child's needs aside, you must take responsibility for what you do, too

Parents need to be aware of the impact of their own behaviour. And, believe me, the consequences are increasingly serious, because toddlers quickly become proficient at manipulating their parents.

Your perspective about your child's nature can determine how well you deal with it

Of course, some children are more difficult than others, and it's also a well-documented fact that a child's personality can influence a parent's actions and reactions; still perspective means everything.

Who Is Your Toddler?

Temperament determines your child's ability to handle unfamiliar tasks and circumstances, her 'firsts'. So, to understand your toddler I have devised a test to help guide your decisions.

Get two clean pieces of paper and, working independently, both you and your partner should reply to the questionnaire opposite.

If you're a single parent, ask the help of another caretaker, the child's grandparents or a good friend who knows your toddler well. That way, you at least have another pair of eyes and can compare notes. No two people see the same child exactly the same way, nor does any child act the same way with two different people.

There are no right or wrong answers here – this is a fact-finding exercise, so don't argue if your answers are different. Simply allow for a broader view. The goal is to help you understand your toddler's make-up.

Keep in mind that this is just an exercise to help you tune in and become more observant about your child's natural inclinations. Mark the answers that reflect your toddler's most typical behaviour – the way she usually acts or reacts.

1. As a baby, my child
   A. rarely cried
   B. cried only when she was hungry, tired or overstimulated
   C. often cried for no apparent reason
   D. cried very loudly, and if I didn't attend to her, it quickly turned into a rage cry
   E. cried angrily, usually when we veered from our usual routine or from what she expected

2. When he wakes up in the morning, my toddler
   A. rarely cries – he plays in his cot until I come in
   B. coos and looks around until he gets bored
   C. needs immediate attention, or he starts crying
   D. screams for me to come in
   E. whimpers to let me know he's up

3. Thinking back to her first bath, I remember that my child
    A. took to the water like a duck
    B. was a little surprised at the sensation but liked it almost immediately
    C. was very sensitive, she shook a little and seemed afraid
    D. was wild-flailing about and splashing
    E. hated it and cried

4. My child's body language has been typically
    A. relaxed almost always, even as a baby
    B. relaxed most of the time, even as a baby
    C. tense and very reactive to external stimuli
    D. jerky – as a baby, his arms and legs often flailed all over the place
    E. rigid – as a baby, his arms and legs were often fairly stiff

5. When I made the transition from liquids to solid food, my toddler
    A. had no problem
    B. adjusted fairly well, as long as I gave her time to adapt to each new taste and texture
    C. scrunched up her face or her lip quivered, as if to say, 'What the Dickens is this?'
    D. dived right in, as if she had been eating solid foods her whole life

    E. grabbed the spoon and insisted on holding it herself

6. When interrupted from an activity he's involved in, my toddler
    A. stops easily
    B. sometimes cries but can be cajoled into a new activity
    C. cries for several minutes before he recovers
    D. wails and kicks and throws himself on the floor
    E. cries as if his heart were breaking

7. My toddler displays anger by
    A. whimpering, but she can be quickly consoled or easily distracted
    B. displaying obvious signs (clenched fist, grimace or crying) and needs reassurance to get through it
    C. having a meltdown like it's the end of the world
    D. being out of control, often tending to throw things
    E. being aggressive, often tending to push or shove

8. In social situations with another child or children, such as a play date, my toddler
    A. is happy and actively involved
    B. gets involved, but every now and then gets upset with other children

C. whines or cries easily, especially when another child grabs his toy

D. runs around a lot and gets involved in everything

E. doesn't want to be involved, stays on the sidelines

9. At nap or bedtimes, the sentence that best describes my toddler is

A. she could sleep through a nuclear blast

B. she is restless before falling asleep but responds well to a gentle pat or reassuring words

C. she is easily disturbed by noises in the house or outside the window

D. she has to be coaxed into bed – she's afraid of missing something

E. she has to have total quiet to go to sleep, or she begins to cry inconsolably

10. When brought to a new house or unfamiliar setting, my toddler

A. adapts easily, smiles and quickly engages

B. needs a little time to adapt, gives a smile but turns away quickly

C. is easily distressed, hides behind me or buries himself in my clothes

D. jumps straight in, but doesn't quite know what to do with himself

   E. tends to balk and get angry, or may go off by
       himself

11. If my toddler is engaged with a particular toy and another
    child wants to join in, she
    A. notices, but stays focused on what she's doing
    B. finds it hard to stay focused once the other child
        catches her eye
    C. gets upset and cries easily
    D. immediately wants whatever the other child is
        playing with
    E. prefers playing alone and often cries if other
        children invade her space

12. When I leave the room, my toddler
    A. shows concern initially, but resumes playing
    B. may show concern but usually doesn't mind unless
        he's tired or sick
    C. cries immediately and looks forlorn
    D. hotfoots after me
    E. cries loudly and lifts up his hands

13. When we come home from any kind of outing, my toddler
    A. settles in easily and immediately
    B. takes a few minutes to get acclimatised
    C. tends to be very fussy

D. is often overstimulated and hard to calm down
E. acts angry and miserable

14. The most noticeable thing about my toddler is how
    A. incredibly well behaved and adaptable she is
    B. how much she has developed precisely on schedule, doing just what the books said she would at each stage
    C. sensitive she is to everything
    D. aggressive she is
    E. grouchy she can be

15. When we go to family gatherings where there are adults and/or children my child knows, my toddler
    A. scopes out the situation, but usually gets right into the swing of things
    B. needs just a few minutes to adapt to the situation, especially if there are a lot of people
    C. is shy, stays close to me, if not on my lap, and might even cry
    D. jumps right into the centre of the action, especially with other children
    E. will join in when he's ready, unless I push him, and then he becomes reluctant

16. At a restaurant, my toddler
    A. is good as gold
    B. can stay seated at the table for around 30 minutes
    C. is easily frightened if the place is crowded and loud, or if strangers talk to her
    D. refuses to sit at the table for more than 10 minutes, unless she's eating
    E. can sit up to 15 or 20 minutes, but needs to leave when she's finished eating

17. A comment that best describes my toddler is
    A. you hardly know there's a little one in the house
    B. he's easy to handle, easy to predict
    C. he's a very delicate child
    D. he's into everything – I can't take my eyes off him when he's out of the cot or playpen
    E. he's very serious – he seems to hold back and ponder things a lot

18. The comment that best describes communication between my toddler and me, since she was a baby, is
    A. she has always let me know exactly what she needs
    B. most of the time her cues are easy
    C. she cries often, which is confusing
    D. she asserts her likes and dislikes very clearly, physically and often loudly
    E. she often gets my attention with loud, angry crying

19. When I nappy or dress my toddler, he
    A. is usually cooperative
    B. sometimes needs a distraction in order to lie still
    C. gets upset and sometimes cries, especially if I try to rush him
    D. balks because he hates to lie or sit still
    E. gets upset if I take too long

20. The type of activity or toy that my toddler likes best is
    A. almost anything that gives her results, like simple building toys
    B. an age-appropriate toy
    C. single-task activities that aren't too loud or stimulating
    D. anything she can bash or use to make a loud noise
    E. almost anything, as long as no one interferes with her

To score the self-test above, write A, B, C, D and E on a piece of paper and, next to each one, count how many times you've used each letter, which denotes a corresponding type.

As   Angel baby
Bs   Textbook baby
Cs   Touchy baby
Ds   Spirited baby
Es   Grumpy baby

Hello, Toddler!

Be sure to read all five descriptions. Even if one doesn't fit your child, reading about all the types might help you understand other children, relatives or playmates who are part of your toddler's social circle.

Angel
Usually very social, this child is immediately comfortable in groups and can fit into most situations. She often develops language earlier than her peers or at least is clearer when making her needs known. When she wants something she can't have, it's fairly easy to distract her before her emotions escalate.

Textbook
You could say this toddler does everything by the book. He's generally pleasant in social situations but can be shy at first with strangers. He's most comfortable in his own environment, but if outings are planned well, and you give him sufficient time and preparation, he won't have much trouble adapting to new surroundings. This is a child who loves routine and likes to know what's coming next.

Touchy
True to her baby self, this little one is sensitive and typically slow to adapt to new situations. She likes the world ordered and knowable. She hates to be interrupted when engrossed. A touchy toddler may not do well in social gatherings, especially if she feels pushed, and she often has difficulty sharing.

Spirited
Our most active toddler, she's very physical, often wilful and may be prone to temper tantrums. This child is the consummate adventurer; she will have a go at anything and is very determined. She displays a great sense of achievement when she accomplishes something. At the same time, she needs very clear boundaries. A spirited toddler can become a leader and very accomplished in whatever area interests her.

Grumpy

He's obstinate and needs things to be his way. He likes his own company best: he's great at independent play. However, he may lack the staying power needed to learn or complete a task and is therefore easily frustrated. These toddlers tend to be insightful, resourceful and creative, and sometimes even wise, acting as if they've been here before.

You probably recognised your toddler in the above descriptions. Maybe he's a cross between two types. In either case, this information is meant to guide and enlighten you, not to alarm you. Your job as a parent is to structure the environment to minimise the pitfalls and bolster the benefits of your child's nature.

Nature or Toddlerhood?

The one constant of toddlerhood is change. Because they're perpetually growing, exploring and testing, toddlers are transformed literally every day. Yours may be cooperative one moment, obstinate the next. Sometimes he gets dressed without any fuss, sometimes you have to chase him. He may eat with gusto on Friday, pick at his food on Saturday. At such trying times, you may *think* that your toddler's personality has changed, but your little one is simply in the process of yet another huge developmental leap. The best way to ride these waves of change is to not make too much of them. Your child isn't having a setback or changing for the worse. It's all part of his growing up.

Accepting Your Toddler

Knowing your toddler's type is not enough; it's also important to accept what you know. I've isolated several reasons why this doesn't always happen:

Performance anxiety

I can't believe the numbers of young women today who seem to have performance anxiety about their parenting. When their child does not behave to perfection they deduce that it's something they as parents did wrong. Feeling bad about yourself doesn't translate into good parenting. Aiming for perfection is impossible and it seems that when parents ease off a bit, then the toddler generally becomes more manageable.

Perfectionism

Perfectionism is performance anxiety taken to the extreme. This trait often results in the parent putting more energy into trying to control their toddler than into listening and observing him.

Signs of Denial

Parents who have trouble accepting their children for who they are tend to make certain kinds of statements. Pay attention to what you *really* mean if you hear yourself saying …

* *'It's a stage – she'll grow out of it.'* Is that reality or a wish? You might have to keep waiting.

* *'Oh, you're fine.'* Are you trying to cajole your toddler out of feelings?

* *'Once he starts talking he'll be easier to handle.'* Development can modify behaviour, but it rarely overrides temperament altogether.

* *'Oh, she won't always be shy.'* But she might always have trouble in new situations.

* *'I wish he were …'* or *'Why can't he be more …'* or *'He used to …'* or *'When will he …'* Whatever words you fill in, it might mean you don't truly accept who he is.

* *'I'm sorry she's so …'* When parents apologise for a child, no matter what he's doing, they're giving him the message that it's not okay to be himself. I can imagine the child ending up in a psychologist's office saying, 'I was never allowed to be myself.'

Instead of her holding on to the illusion that your toddler will change, things tend to improve when parents accept their toddler's nature and start to make fewer excuses for their behaviour.

Voices in – and out of – your head

Some parents can't see clearly because they are haunted by other people's opinions and expectations-real or imagined.

Plagued by childhood

Parents almost can't help identifying with their children; it's a natural process. Problems arise, though, when such connections override the child's own individuality.

Bad fit

The idea that some parents and children are a 'bad fit' is not a new one.

I suggest that parents like this slooooow down and accept the toddler they have.

How to See More Clearly

You may have recognised yourself in one of the descriptions of parents who have trouble accepting their children's temperament.

If so, here's a helpful checklist to improve your sensitivity and powers of observation.

- Self-reflection. Look at who *you* are, both as a child and an adult. Be aware of your own temperament and of the tapes that run in your head.

- Join a group to see how other children act and react. It's important to watch other children and to observe the interaction between your child and others.

- Remember that some voices are worth listening to. Talk with other parents whom you respect. Listen to their observations about your child with an open mind. Don't see everything as a put-down – and don't get defensive.

- Make believe it's someone else's child – what do you *really* see? Step back. Be as objective as you possibly can. You'll be doing your child and yourself a big favour.

- Have a plan for change. Take steps to give your child what he or she uniquely needs. Remember that changes take time.

A Plan for Change

If you see yourself in any of these descriptions, if you hear yourself making certain kinds of statements (see box on page 21), you may be having a bit of trouble accepting your child as he or she really is. If so, you need a plan:

1. Take a step back. Honestly look at your child. Have you been ignoring or underestimating her temperament? Think back to when she was a baby. You'll find threads of her personality that you probably noticed from the day she was born. Pay attention to this information, instead of pushing it away.

2. Accept what you see. Don't just give lip service to the idea of loving the child you have – really embrace who your child is.

3. Look at what you've been doing that works against your child's temperament. What actions, reactions, things you've said? For example, do you give your Grumpy child enough space? Do you talk too loudly or move too fast for your Touchy toddler? Do you provide enough activity for your Spirited child?

4. Change your own behaviour and structure the environment to meet your child's needs. Of course, change takes time. Also, I can't give you a precise road map, because your child is unique. In the next chapter, though, I offer H.E.L.P., a good strategy that will enable you to walk that narrow line, respecting your child for who he is and, at the same time, providing the structure and boundaries within which he can thrive.

CHAPTER TWO
Behaviour

Just as I don't believe there are 'bad' children – only children who haven't been taught how to behave and interact socially – I don't believe there are 'bad' mums or dads.

H.E.L.P. – An Overview

I'm fond of acronyms, because they help parents keep certain principles in mind. I've come up with one that will remind you of four factors that help create and nurture the parent/child bond, keep your toddler out of harm's way and, at the same time, foster your little one's growth and independence. I call it H.E.L.P., and it stands for:

Hold yourself back
Encourage exploration
Limit
Praise

Good News about Attachment

For most children, the primary 'attachment figure' is Mum, although anyone who provides continuous and consistent physical and emotional care, and demonstrates an emotional investment in a child, can also become an attachment figure. These various people are not interchangeable, as anyone who has lost a beloved nanny quickly finds out, and the most recent research indicates that one doesn't detract from or undermine the other. In other words, Mum, don't worry. Though your toddler spends all day with Dad or another caretaker, she'll still run to you when you walk in and want you to kiss her bruise.

Now let's talk in greater detail about each of the letters in H.E.L.P.

The H – Why Hold Back?

Clearly, some children want and need their parent or other caretaker to interact with them. But the only way to determine this is to hold back and observe your child's patterns. Watch, and you'll find out. Whatever you see, I urge you not to think of yourself as the choreographer of your child's life. A parent's role is to support, not lead. Here are some suggestions that will help you to hold back.

Let your child take the lead

If it's a new plaything, let her operate the toy before you do. If it's a new situation or place, let her climb down from your lap or let go of your hand in her own time. If it's a new person, let her hold out her arms when she's ready, not when you are. When she asks for your help, of course be there for her, but give her only as much assistance as she needs, rather than taking over.

Let situations unfold naturally

As you observe your child, your mind might buzz with possibilities: 'Oh, I'm sure he's not going to like that toy,' or 'He's going to be afraid if that dog comes too close.' But don't jump to conclusions or second-guess your toddler. Yesterday's tastes and fears may not be the same as today's.

Get out of the way

Everyone hates a busybody or a know-it-all, including toddlers. Naturally, you know how to stack blocks without their falling. Of course, you know an 'easier' way to get something down from the shelf. You're the grown-up! Equally important, if you do it for him, he won't learn to problem solve. Interference tells your child he can't do it – a message that will stick with him and impact on the way he views all new challenges in the future.

Don't compare your child to other children

Allow her to develop in her own time. I know, I know, this can be difficult, especially if a mother sitting next to you in the park compares her child with yours ('Oh, I see that Annie is still crawling'). Your child will pick up your anxiety almost as fast as it comes over you. And put yourself in her place.

Remember that you are not your child

Don't project your feelings or fears on to her. It's true that sometimes the apple doesn't fall far from the tree, but allow your toddler to develop without prejudice. If you hear yourself making statements such as, 'I never liked large groups either,' or 'Her father was shy, too,' you might be over-identifying with your toddler's struggles. Empathy is good, but the way to express it is to wait for your child to tell you (by words or actions) what she's feeling. Then you can say, 'I know what you mean.'

The E – That Fine Line between Encouragement and Rescue

The bottom line here is that we don't step in until our child needs us. Knowing your child provides important clues.

A guide to stepping in

Be an observant, respectful, H.E.L.P.ing parent by being patient, giving your child ample opportunity to explore, choosing age-appropriate toys and guiding him towards activities. Follow this protocol for stepping in:

- Know what your child sounds and looks like when frustrated; hold yourself back and observe him until you see those signs.

- Start with verbal observation: 'I can see that you're having a problem.'

- Always ask before actually helping: 'Would you like me to give you a hand?'

- Respect your child if he says, 'no', or 'I can do it myself', even if it means letting him go outside without a coat. This is how children learn.

- Remember that your child actually knows more than you think he does – for instance, when he's cold, wet, hungry, tired, or has had enough of a particular activity or place. Cajoling or trying to convince him otherwise will eventually make him doubt his own perceptions.

Know what frustration looks like on your child
Rely on facial expressions and body language.

Know your child's tolerance level
Some types of children have more perseverance than others, more patience and, therefore, a higher tolerance for frustration.

Know what your child is developmentally capable of
You need to ask yourself, 'Is my toddler ready for this activity?'

More about the E – creating encouraging environments
Toddlers, especially, are filled with wonder. They're little scientists in the making. Their eyes and minds are wide open and ready to explore. They don't need an object to stimulate them.

So when you focus on the E in H.E.L.P., scale back a bit. The raw materials for a rich educational environment are already at your fingertips. Encourage your child to explore the ordinary things in his environment, to observe the natural wonders of nature and allow his growing mind to consider, create and construct.

The L – Living with Limits

Your little darling doesn't yet understand the rules of life, and it's up to you to teach him. This is where the L in H.E.L.P. is useful. Toddlers need boundaries. You can't give them carte blanche because they don't have the mental or emotional ability to deal with such wide-open freedom. We also need to stress the difference between us and them: we are the adults – and we know better. Below are some pointers:

Limit stimulation
Limiting stimulation is particularly important for any child as you near her bedtime hour.

Limit choice
Giving limited choice helps a child feel as if he has some control over his world, but too many choices are confusing and counterproductive.

Limit undesirable behaviour
Children need to learn what's expected of them. The only way that happens is when parents teach them.

Limit anything that's not good in big doses
For most children, television and sweets would be at the top of this list.

Limit potential failure
Although your toddler's abilities are growing every day, don't try to push her. By giving her a toy that's too advanced for her, by expecting her to sit through a movie that's too long, or eat in a posh restaurant that isn't kid-friendly, you're not only putting your child in over her head, you're asking for trouble.

Limit your own uncivilised behaviour
Toddlers develop skills by repetition and imitation. During every waking hour, your toddler is watching, listening and learning from your example. It behoves you to pay attention, therefore, to what you're inadvertently 'teaching' him.

If the above list makes you feel as if you have to be a referee or a policeman all the time, to some extent, you're accurate. Toddlers cry out for boundaries. Otherwise, their interior landscape and the world at large is too scary and unmanageable.

The P – In Praise of Praise

By far, the most positive teaching comes from affection and praise for a job well done.

Even the scientists agree that love is the magical element in the parenting equation. When a child feels loved, she feels secure, she wants to please her parents and, as she gets older, she wants to do right by the world as well.

The trick is to praise only for a job well done. Ask yourself, 'Did my child really do something worthy of praise?' Otherwise, your kind words will mean nothing and do nothing, and she will eventually tune out your praise. Remember, too, that the purpose of praise is not to make your child feel good the way hugs and kisses do. It is to reinforce a task well done, to compliment good manners and to acknowledge good social skills, including sharing, kindness and cooperation.

Everyday H.E.L.P. – A Checklist

Keep H.E.L.P. in the back of your mind throughout the day, especially if you find yourself in a sticky situation. Of course, with a toddler that could happen several times a day! Think of each letter and ask yourself . . .

H: Am I holding back or have I been in my child's face, interfering, being too intrusive, rescuing before he needs my help? Remember that the H – holding back – is for the purpose of observation, which is not the same as being detached, rejecting or ignoring your toddler.

E: Have I encouraged my child to explore or do I hover? There are many opportunities in a day for exploration, any number of which can be thwarted by a parent. Do you, for instance, talk for her when she's playing quietly with another child? Do you do her puzzles instead of seeing if she can manage them on her own? Do you stack blocks for her without first letting her try? Are you constantly directing, monitoring and instructing?

L: Do I limit or allow things to go too far? Too much of anything is not usually good for toddlers. Do you give too many choices or allow too much stimulation? Do you wait too long before reining in tantrums, aggressiveness or other high emotions? Do you curtail activities that aren't good in big doses, like eating sweets or watching television? And do you allow your child to participate in situations that aren't age-appropriate, which could lead to danger, distress or feelings of failure?

P: Do I praise appropriately or do I overpraise? Do I use praise appropriately – to reinforce specific acts of cooperation, kindness or behaviour, or a job well done? I've seen parents who say 'Good job' to their toddler when the child just sits there and breathes. Not only are those parents using praise improperly, but eventually their words of praise, deserved or otherwise, will mean nothing to their children.

CHAPTER THREE

R&R – Routines and Rituals

First let me explain what I mean by R&R. Throughout this chapter, I tend to use the words 'ritual' and 'routine' interchangeably because the two Rs are intertwined. Indeed, whenever you repeat and reinforce an act, you are doing R&R.

Why Do Children Need R&R?

R&R provides security

A toddler's world is challenging, confusing, and often scary. R&R gives your child support as she takes her tentative first steps, bolstering her both in the physical sense and in understanding and managing her emotions and her new social life as well.

R&R cuts down on toddler struggles

I'm not saying that we can eliminate the inevitable tug-of-war altogether, but instituting predictable mealtime, bedtime and play routines will surely diminish the battles.

R&R helps toddlers deal with separation
That's because R&R helps children anticipate events that repeat daily. We can use this knowledge to teach toddlers that even though Mum leaves, she'll return.

R&R supports all kinds of learning – physical feats, emotional control and social behaviour
Children learn by repetition and imitation. R&R helps shape children, teaching them not just skills, but morals, values and mutual respect.

R&R avoids problems by helping parents set clear boundaries and be consistent
R&R helps us structure situations and lay out expectations ahead of time – in which case we're less likely to find we have an out-of-control toddler to cope with.

R&R helps you prepare your child for new experiences
The idea is to introduce your little one to new experiences at home first, increase the challenges bit by bit and then take the show on the road.

R&R allows everyone to slow down and to turn the most mundane moments into times of connection
If we parents slow ourselves down and imbue everyday events with intention ('I will use bedtime to connect with my child'),

we are also teaching our children by example how to put greater meaning into everyday moments.

R&R Around the Clock

Let me remind you that while certain types of R&R are practised by almost every family I know – a book or story before bedtime – R&R must be tailored to your family.

The mainstays of family life are: waking, eating, bathing, exits and entrances, clean-up, nap and bedtimes. You won't find any problem-solving ideas here; this chapter is about prevention. By repetition of these acts, by teaching children what you expect, you can often avoid problems before they occur.

Waking up
There are only two ways a toddler wakes up – happy or crying. In infancy, waking patterns are determined by temperament. But by the time babies become toddlers, their waking patterns are more a matter of what parents have reinforced and less the child's personality. In fact, good R&R can actually override temperament.

My Toddler Wakes Up Crying: What's Happening?

When a parent tells me their toddler wakes up crying, it usually suggests that the child doesn't feel comfortable in her own cot. I usually ask these questions:

- Do you tend to rush in at the first sound she makes? You may have inadvertently trained her to cry when you don't come fast enough.

- Does she also display anxiety – wailing at the top of her lungs, wrapping her arms tightly around you when you come to get her? This is a sure sign that the cot has become a dreaded place. Take steps to change that (see this page).

- Does she have periods during the day when she enjoys playing in her cot? If not, it might be a good idea to include them in your play routine.

Intention

To teach your child that bed is a nice place to hang out and to have a toddler who wakes up smiling.

Preparation

Make sure your child plays in his cot during the day. Spending fun time in a cot reinforces the idea not only that it's safe, but it's a great place to play.

From beginning to end

In the morning, try to gauge how long it takes your child to go from cooing and playing on her own to crying. Walk in before she gets to the crying stage. The ritual ends with your taking her out of the cot, with both of you excited to start the day.

Whatever you do, don't give your child sympathy if he cries in the morning. Pick him up, hug him, but please don't say, 'Oh, you poor thing!' Act jolly, as if you're happy to start the day. Remember that children learn by imitation.

Mealtimes

Toddlers are notoriously fussy eaters – a fact that concerns many parents who consult me.

Intention

Think of meals as a way of teaching your toddler what it means to sit at a table, use utensils, try new foods and, most important, eat with the family.

Preparation

Serve meals at approximately the same time every day. Allow your toddler to participate in family dinners at eight to ten months. If you have older children, have them eat at the same time.

From beginning to end

Hand washing is an ideal premeal ritual that lets a child know it's time to eat. Start the meal with grace, candlelighting, or simply saying, 'You may begin.' Have conversation, just as you would at a dinner with adults. Consider the meal over when your child stops eating. Remember the intention of this ritual: to teach your child mealtime mores. One doesn't play while eating.

End the meal with whatever practice feels right for your family. Some families say a final prayer or blow out the candles. I also like to get children in the habit of toothbrushing after meals. Start as soon as you've introduced solid foods.

To get your child used to the idea of brushing her teeth, start with her gums. Wrap a soft, clean terrycloth around your index finger and rub her gums after eating. That way, when her teeth come in, she'll be accustomed to the feeling. Buy a soft, baby toothbrush. Your toddler will probably suck on it at first, but eventually she'll learn how to brush.

Follow-up

Keep up mealtime R&R no matter where you go.

Bath Time

As much as some infants dread a bath, toddlers often dread getting out of the tub. A consistent bath-time ritual can go a long way towards avoiding that struggle.

Intention

If it's an evening bath, the intention is to help your toddler relax and get ready for bed. If it's a morning bath, which is less frequent among families I know, the purpose is to get your toddler ready for the day.

Preparation

Announce to your toddler in a cheery voice, 'It's time for your bath!'

Always run your cold water tap first and then add the hot. To prevent your toddler from accidentally turning on the hot water and scalding himself, buy a cover that goes over the hot water tap, or, if it's a two-in-one handle, one that goes over the whole apparatus. Also, use a rubber bath mat to prevent slipping, and set the thermostat on your hot water heater at no higher than 52°C/125°F.

From beginning to end

I always like to sing a song while bathing. 'This is the way we wash our arms, wash our arms, wash our arms. This is the way we wash our arms, so early in the evening. This is the way we wash our back, wash our back,' and so on. Because most toddlers hate to see a bath end, don't lift her straight out of the tub. Instead, start taking the toys out of the tub first. Then pull the plug, let the water out and say, 'Uh-oh, water's going down the drain. Bath time is over!' End with a good snuggle in a fluffy towel.

Even though you may have more confidence in your child's ability now that she's a toddler, under no circumstances should you ever leave her alone in the bath.

Exits and Entrances

All children go through a stage when it's hard for them to separate from their parents, even if Mum just goes into the next room to make dinner.

Intention

To make your child feel secure, knowing that when you leave, you'll also return.

Preparation

Introduce your child to the idea of your leaving. If you start around six months and proceed gradually, by eight months he will probably play on his own for up to 40 minutes. Each time you exit, say the words, 'I'm going to [the kitchen/my room]. I'll be there if you need me.' But come right back when the child calls you, so that he learns he can trust you. When you do leave the house, whether you're going on an errand for 15 minutes or to a full day of work, be honest. Don't say, 'I'll be right back,' if you're planning to be gone for five hours, or worse, 'I'll be back in five minutes.'

From beginning to end

When you leave, use the same words and gestures each time. 'I'm going to work, honey bun,' accompanied by a big hug and kiss. Remember, it's often not the leaving that upsets a child; it's how you leave. If you keep going back and forth, you're reinforcing the child's anxiety. You're telling her (indirectly): 'Your crying will bring me back to you.'

For your own peace of mind: if your child is upset when you leave, call the sitter from your car or when you get to work. I assure you, most children are fine within five minutes after Mum exits.

When you return, walk into the house saying the same words each time: 'I'm back,' or 'Hi, honey, I'm hoooome.'

Never bring a gift home when you return. You are the gift.

Clean-up
Because toddlers often have trouble with transitions, I like to incorporate clean-up routines throughout the day. In my groups, for example, even with children as young as eight months, we always had 'clean-up' before doing music, which was a more settled activity. Besides, it's never too early to start learning responsibility and respect.

Intention
To teach a child responsibility and to instil in him respect for his own and other people's belongings.

Preparation
Your toddler should have a box, several hooks and, if possible, some shelves in a cupboard that she can reach on her own.

From beginning to end
When your child comes into the house, say, 'Time to hang our jackets.' You go to the cupboard and hang yours, and he will follow suit. After he has been playing in his room, and it's time to either eat or get ready for a nap or bed, say, 'Time to clean up now.' At first you'll have to help.

Follow-up
Wherever your toddler goes, whether it's to Grandma's, to a play group or to cousin Nell's, reinforce this clean-up ritual.

Naps and Bedtime
There's nothing quite so delicious as book reading and snuggle time before bed. Parents usually love it as much as toddlers do. Then comes the moment of getting your child off to sleep. Some children need more support than others – sleep is a skill children must learn.

Intention
At naptime and in the evening, your goal is to help your child calm down, going from the rigours and excitement of play to a more relaxed state.

Preparation
End stimulating activities, like TV or play. Put toys away (see the preceding clean-up ritual) and announce, 'It's almost time for bed.' Draw the curtains and pull down the blinds. To help your child relax physically, incorporate the evening bath as part of the night time ritual – as well as massage if your child enjoys it.

From beginning to end

After bath and jammies, say, 'Let's go and choose a book.' Decide ahead of time how many books you're willing to read (or how many times you'll read the same one) and tell her. Stick to it – otherwise, you're asking for trouble.

Beyond the above givens, families tend to tailor this ritual to their and their children's taste.

Special-occasion R&R

As I said at the outset of this book, innumerable occasions arise in a family's day, week or year that can be enhanced by conscious rituals. As with everyday rituals, an important aspect is personal meaning. What works for one family may seem empty to another. Below are some of the most common special occasions.

Family 'Togetherness' Time

Whether you do it once a week or once a month, it's important to have regular times of togetherness in a family, a time when you can share ideas, emotions, or simply have time for fun.

Intention

To foster cooperation, communication and connection.

Preparation

If you have children four or older in addition to a toddler, you might want to make this into a more formal 'family meeting' ritual, which allows for sharing and forgiveness, as well as fun activities. If it's just you, your partner and your toddler, simply set aside a few hours a week during which you are all together.

From beginning to end

Start with an announcement: 'This is our special family time.' Light a candle to signify the ritual's beginning, taking care to keep the flame out of your toddler's reach. Even if you don't embark on a full-blown family meeting, you can still designate this as 'sacred' time and space that neither responsibilities nor concerns can invade. Don't compromise this ritual by answering phones, attending to chores around the house, or dealing with adult matters. This is a time to be with your toddler – it can be a meal, a trip to the park, or an hour or two in the living room, talking, playing, singing songs (hopefully, not watching TV). Blow the candle out to signify the end.

Follow-up

By repeating this family togetherness ritual, your child will not only come to understand its importance, but also look forward to it.

Dad Time

In families where the children have a more equal balance of parent time, it's because Dad makes a real effort to spend separate time with his child or children, and Mum supports him in it. Toddlerhood is often the first time they really feel comfortable as caretakers.

Intention

To help a child have a separate connection with his father.

Preparation

Some planning and even negotiating may be necessary between Mum and Dad, especially if both parents are working. Iron out kinks in the schedule ahead of time. Once Dad commits to this time, however, nothing should stand in his way.

From beginning to end

Let the child know that this is her special time with Dad. As always, saying the same words and doing the same things each time help mark the beginning of this ritual.

Daddy time needn't always be playtime, though. It's good for Dad to take over aspects of the daily routine as well. Most popular among fathers seems to be the evening bath. Other men love to cook breakfast. The point is, just about anything can be Dad time as long as it's Dad's intention to make it a regular, recurring event.

Making It Hard for Dad

Many mothers can unintentionally compromise their toddler's comfort with their fathers because they:

- *Tell Dad what to think:* Greta and Dad are playing with a toy vacuum. 'She doesn't want to play with that now,' Mum says. 'We'd already put it away.' It's important for Dad to establish what Greta wants and doesn't want to do.

- *Criticise Dad in front of their child:* 'That's not how to put her T-shirt on.'

- *Send the child a message that it's not safe to be with Dad:* she hovers when Dad is with Greta. If Greta cries, she immediately 'rescues' her from Dad.

- *Make him the bad guy:* whenever Greta won't go to sleep, Mum sends Dad in to settle her down. When Greta misbehaves, Mum says, 'Wait 'til your daddy gets home.'

- *Are reluctant to give up the nurturing role:* Dad is reading a story to Greta, and Mum comes in, picks her off Dad's lap and says, 'Oh, I'll finish the story.'

Family Milestones

Birthdays, anniversaries and other special family days are all good reasons to celebrate. But here are two points of caution: don't overwhelm your toddler with a too big or too fancy or otherwise inappropriate celebration, and don't limit your celebrations to events in which your toddler is the star. In other words, it's good for even young children to step out of the limelight and learn how to honour other people, too.

Intention
To help your toddler understand the significance of a particular milestone without the usual emphasis on material acquisitions.

Preparation
A few days before the event, let your toddler know that a 'big day' is coming. If the occasion is his birthday, invite only a few close relatives. A good rule of thumb is to have one friend per year of age. So if your toddler is turning two, invite two pals.

From beginning to end
When parents of a one-year-old throw a big barbecue, I know it's more for them than for their child. The best child-centred birthday parties are loosely structured and short. They begin with free play, ending with food and cake and the blowing out of candles. No matter what the occasion is, though, try to limit the celebration to two hours. Remember toddlers don't need entertaining. The purpose here is not only to celebrate milestones, but to give children a sense of family connection, and to begin helping them learn manners and generosity.

Holidays
I suggest that you try to make these times less materialistic. Admittedly, it's not easy to battle the rampant materialism of our culture.

Intention
To place more of an emphasis on the reason for the celebration and less on the presents one gets.

Preparation
Buy a picture book that explains the festival and read it to your child. Think of ways that your child can participate other than by getting gifts – decorating, making presents for other people, helping to make cookies.

From beginning to end
When children are brought up with spiritual values, they become surprisingly sensitive to the needs of others.

R&R Forever

Parents who create rituals and routines for their children describe them as an 'anchor' for daily life and for their own values.

CHAPTER FOUR
Striding Towards Independence

Milestones aren't really accomplishments. Rather, each is Nature's way of saying, 'Pay attention: your baby is getting ready for the next step.' A large variety of behaviour and growth patterns exist within 'normal' ranges of development. The truth is, by the time children are three, they all pretty much do the same thing – no matter what their parents have done for them. (So much for head starts.) Development follows what I call a natural progression – it automatically happens. Some children develop faster than others physically, while others make quicker mental or emotional strides. Whatever path they take, they are

No Showing Off

'Watch,' Proud Mother said to her out-of-town guests. 'He can clap now.' Then, when the poor little dear just sat there, she said dejectedly, 'Oh, he did it this morning.'

Children are not circus performers. Parents shouldn't ask them to do tricks for their grandparents or for adult friends. Proud Mother's son may not have understood his mum's words, but he surely heard her tone of voice and saw the disappointment on her face when he didn't respond on cue.

Children do exactly what they can do, *when* they can do it. If they can clap, they'll clap. They don't purposely hold back. By asking your child to do something he might have done once, you're setting him up for failure and disappointment. And if by chance he does perform on cue, he may get applause, but then you're appreciating him for how well he does tricks rather than applauding who he is.

probably following in their parents' footsteps, because rate and pattern of development is largely a genetic phenomenon. It means that you have to be an observant guide, rather than a pushy teacher.

H.E.L.P.

Hold yourself back: wait for your child to show signs of readiness before rushing in.

Encourage exploration: give your child opportunities according to her readiness – so that she attempts new challenges and stretches her repertoire.

Limit: stay within his 'learning triangle' (see page 62), taking care never to allow your child to attempt something that leads to extreme frustration, a heightened emotional state, or danger.

Praise: applaud a job well done, a new skill mastered and admirable behaviour, but never go overboard.

Your Toddler on the Loose

The driving force of toddlerhood is mobility. Your little one is on the go and wants to keep going.

> If your child falls, don't rush in without first judging whether he's really hurt. Your anxiety can hurt him, too – by scaring him and shattering his self-confidence.

The Crawling Conundrum

It has long been recognised that some children go straight from sitting to standing. Today, their ranks are growing. The reason, scientists believe, is that now babies spend less time on their tummies, a by-product of concern about Sudden Infant Death Syndrome (SIDS).

Prior to 1994 when the 'Back to Sleep' campaign was launched, most babies were put to sleep face down, and wanting a better view of the world, they learned to flip over – a precursor to crawling. But now that parents are routinely advised to put babies to sleep on their backs, little ones don't need to flip from front to back.

Two recent studies, one in the United States and one in England, conclude that many back-sleepers (one-third in the US study) don't roll over or crawl on schedule and some skip the crawling stage altogether. But don't worry if your child is one of them. By 18 months, there are virtually no developmental differences between crawlers and non-crawlers – and both start walking at the same age. Nor is there any validity to the once-held belief that crawling is necessary for brain development.

Spurts of unprecedented mobility often cause sleep disturbances. Your child's limbs are alive with movement, much the same way yours are after a workout. She's not used to it. Your toddler may start waking up at night, stand up in her cot and cry out for you because she doesn't yet know how to get down. You'll need to teach her . . . during the day. Put her in her cot for part of an afternoon play period. When she stands up, take her hands, place them on the vertical bars of the cot and, with your hands on top of hers, gently slide them down. As her hands go lower, it will cause her to bend her knees and sit. After only two or three times, she'll get it.

The reality is, toddlers go through phases. Just when you've got used to your child's being one way, he'll do something else. Truth be told, the one and only thing that you can expect from your toddler's life is change. You can't control it, and you can't (and shouldn't want to) stop it. But you can change your attitude towards it.

Milestones of Mobility

Feat	Stages Children Go Through	Tips/Comments
Sitting	If put into position, sits unaided, steadied by her own arms, but balance is precarious; posture is stiff and robotic, like a baby Frankenstein monster minus the stitches.	Place cushions around her for safety.
	Reaches for a toy without falling over.	
	Rotates her body from side to side.	
	Gets herself into a sitting position without anyone's help.	
Crawling	Practises 'swimming' on his tummy and kicking – movements that he'll use in crawling.	
	Figures out that by squirming, he can move himself.	

Feat	Stages Children Go Through	Tips/Comments
	Using his feet to push off, he crawls backwards.	This stage can be very frustrating; if he tries to get a toy, he travels further from it.
	'Creeps' – a kind of forward wriggling motion.	Once he starts moving, make sure electrical outlets are covered and cords out of reach; don't leave a child under two unattended.
	Gets up on all fours and rocks.	
	Finally gets arms and legs to work together.	Children who prefer crawling to walking zoom around the house on all fours. If your child skips this stage, she'll be none the worse for it (see page 53).
Standing	In infancy, exhibits a stiff-legged reflex that then disappears.	

Feat	Stages Children Go Through	Tips/Comments
	In fourth or fifth month, she delights in 'standing' on your lap, your hands securely tucked under her armpits.	
	Pulls herself up.	When she is able to pull herself into a standing position, offer her your fingers to help her be a bit more steady on her feet.
Cruising	Walks holding on to furniture or someone's hands.	If he has been cruising for two months or more and is still not quite confident enough to let go, try moving objects he normally holds on to – say, a chair and a table, a little further apart. Then, in order to keep going, he has to brave that gap on his own.
	Lets go, first with one hand.	

Feat	Stages Children Go Through	Tips/Comments
Toddling	Look, Mum! No hands! Walks tentatively on his own but falls over if he loses momentum.	Once your child starts toddling, keep the floor uncluttered and make sure there are no sharp edges where he can clunk his head. As he gets steadier on his bare feet, encourage him to experiment on different kinds of surfaces – it will improve his motor control.
	Gains increasing control of her muscles and is better able to handle that still-oversized head of hers; she won't have to watch her feet as she toddles.	Keep a careful eye on her at all times, making sure, for instance, that whatever object (chair, pram, push toy) she leans on isn't so light she can tip it over.

Feat	Stages Children Go Through	Tips/Comments
Walking	After a month or so of toddling, logging in several miles of practice can expand his repertoire: • Walks and carries a toy. • Walks and can look up. • Can reach above his head while walking. • Can turn, walk up and down a slope, squat down and get back up with little effort.	Clear the decks. Like Pinocchio, your little one has turned into a real boy! If you have any glass doors, now is the time to cover them with Plexiglas – a child who walks, but still can't stop easily, can run right through a glass door.
You Name It! (Running, jumping, spinning, kicking, dancing, climbing . . .)	She can jump, spin and dance. She runs constantly, even plays 'chase' with her friends.	She has no sense of what's safe and what's not, so you need eyes in the back of your head.
	Tears about the house and attempts to climb into and on to everything.	Give him climbing opportunities but point out what he cannot climb on – like your living room couch.

Building Trust

The dictionary includes the following definitions of 'trust' – confidence, firm belief, reliance, care, consign for care. Each meaning of the word sheds light on various aspects of the parent/child connection. We are the caretakers of our children, and we need to build their trust in us so that they, in turn, can trust themselves.

Trust is a two-way street. Fostering your child's ability to play on her own lets her know that you trust her. But you first must build her trust in you:

* Anticipate change and think about it from the child's perspective.
* Make separations gradual.
* Don't place more responsibility on your child than she can handle.
* Don't ask your child to do things she can't yet achieve.

Playing on Their Own

Play is truly the business of toddlerhood. It's where a great deal of learning and mind stretching take place. Toys and activities must not only be age-appropriate, but also playtimes must be structured to encourage your child to amuse himself independently, and when it's time to do other things, to help him stop playing.

Children need to know how to delineate their play time.

Beginning

Initiate fun time by announcing, 'Now it's time to play.'

Middle

During play periods, keep the number of playthings to a minimum.

End

Toddlers have no concept of time, so it won't do you (or her) any good to say, 'In five minutes, you'll have to stop playing.' Instead, give her a verbal and visual warning. As you take out the toy box for clean-up, say, 'Playtime is almost over.' However, if she's very involved, don't just whisk her away. She might be in the midst of trying to figure out whether the square block fits into the round hole, and you ought to respect her need to finish. At the same time, remember that you're the adult; you have to set boundaries. If your child continues to resist stopping or refuses putting her toys away, acknowledge her feelings, but be firm:

> **Signs of Potential Danger**
> Never leave a child unattended before the age of two. Put him in a cot or playpen, or leave another adult in charge. After the age of two, *if* you know that an area is childproof and you've watched your child playing there before and know he's not prone to dangerous risk taking, trusting him on his own for short periods builds his confidence.

'I can see that you don't want to stop now, but it's dinnertime.' Finally, engage in a clean-up ritual (see pages 43–44).

If you know that your child has trouble leaving an activity or ending a game, set a timer for the end of play period and tell her, 'When the buzzer goes off, we have to [whatever your next activity is: eat, leave for the park, get ready for bed].' When the 'control' belongs to an object, you don't have to assume the unpleasant role of nag.

Clean House!
The numbers of toys in most kids' rooms nowadays is shocking. Besides buying too many in the first place, parents never get rid of toys that are no longer interesting to the child or developmentally appropriate. Put unused toys in the attic for future children or donate them to charity. I prefer the latter, especially if you involve little ones in the process. It's never too early to help children see the benefit of good deeds. Make a ritual out of it, perhaps by making a date every three to six months on your family calendar as 'Toy Giveaway Day'. If you child is too young or too reluctant to help you sort through everything, do it when she's in bed. She probably won't notice that a particular toy is gone. If she does, bring it back – it must have been one of her favourites.

Your Toddler's Learning Triangle

Naturally, play is not just a matter of when but also what. I suggest that parents always stay within their toddler's learning triangle – that is, present physical and mental tasks which the child can manipulate and get pleasure from on his own. Activities and toys should be age-appropriate.

Toddler Safety

The expression 'into everything' sums up toddlerhood. The good news is that almost anything is fascinating to your child. The bad news is that almost anything is fascinating to your child – including electrical outlets, the slot in your VCR, Grandma's delicate figurines, air conditioner vents, animals' eyes, keyholes, bits of dirt, and the contents of the cat-litter tray, to name a few. Thus, while it doesn't take much to amuse your toddler, it takes a lot to keep him safe. Purchase a first-aid kit. Look around you and use your common sense. Here's what to avoid and how to do it:

- Tripping/falling: Keep rooms reasonably uncluttered; place corner guards on sharp corners; install window guards and gates at the top and bottom of stairs; place nonslip mats in the bath or shower and under rugs on bare floors.

- Poisoning: Install safety locks on any cabinets containing medicines or poisonous household substances; even mouthwash and cosmetics should be out of reach. (Your child won't die from eating pet food, but you might want to keep it out of reach, too.) If you think a poisonous substance has been ingested, call your doctor or 999 before doing anything.

- Choking: Remove mobiles from the cot; keep button-sized batteries and anything else that can fit through a toilet paper roll out of reach.

- Strangling: Shorten curtain and blind cords and electrical cords, or use pegs or masking tape to keep them above your child's reach.

- Drowning: Never leave your child alone in the bathroom, and certainly not in the tub, nor in a kiddie pool, or even a bucket; install toilet-seat locks.

- Burning: Keep chairs, foot stools, and ladders away from worktops and cookers; install cooker knob-guards; cover the bath tap with a guard or wrap it with a towel; keep water heaters at 52°C/125°F to avoid scalding.

- Electric shocks: Cover all outlets and make sure every lamp in your house has a bulb in it. I advise all parents to take a CPR course. If you've taken one that focused exclusively on infant emergencies, you need a refresher class on toddlers. Young children require different types of manoeuvres than infants when administering CPR and handling other emergencies – for example, dislodging an object caught in the throat.

Boy Toys? Girl Toys?

I've noticed in my toddler group that mothers of boys – less so mothers of girls – have very definite ideas about what toys are gender-appropriate for their children. For instance, Robby, age 19 months, loved the dolls in the play box, but his mother, Eileen, would invariably intervene when he picked one up. 'That's for little girls, honey.' Poor Robby looked crestfallen. When I asked Eileen about it, she explained that her hubby would be upset if he thought that his son played with dolls.

Rubbish, I say! Just as we encourage children to play with toys that teach them new skills and stretch their minds, we ought to encourage them to go beyond gender stereotypes. When a boy plays with a doll, he learns to be nurturing. When a girl plays with a fire engine, she learns about excitement and activity. Why should either of them be denied a full range of experiences? After all, when today's toddlers grow up, they will need to be both caring *and* capable.

From Feeding to Eating

How it goes depends on three factors: the atmosphere (your attitude towards food and the climate it creates in your home), the eating experience (the social and emotional pleasure – or distress – of mealtimes) and the food (what your child consumes).

I describe each of these elements below. As you read, keep in mind that you control the atmosphere and the eating experience, but life will be a lot easier if you remember that your child controls the food.

The Atmosphere

Parents whose children are 'good eaters' tend to go with the flow. They create an atmosphere of fun and ease at mealtimes. They never force a particular food or insist that a child who isn't hungry continue eating.

> **Feeding Alert!**
> Overanxious parents can turn children into anxiety-ridden non-eaters. It may mean that your child is picking up your concerns about food, or that you're making her stay too long at the table if she:
>
> - Holds food in her mouth without chewing
> - Repeatedly spits food out
> - Gags or vomits

Despite your child's now more active lifestyle, he won't always be in the mood to eat, nor will he necessarily like what you put in front of him. So instead of obsessing over uneaten food, look at your child. If he's alert, active and happy, he's probably getting whatever nutrition he needs.

The Eating Experience

The more your toddler is exposed to the social nature of eating, the better he'll become at sitting still, feeding himself and enjoying the communal occasion.

Start early to include your child

As soon as she can sit up, she's ready to join the family at the dinner table. And the first time she grabs a spoon from you, that's your cue to encourage her to eat on her own.

Dine with him

Even if you're not hungry, have a snack – some cut-up vegetables, a piece of toast – and sit at the table with him. It makes the mealtime more of an interactive process than if you were just sitting there, trying to get food into him. It also takes some of the focus and pressure off him. You're in it together!

Don't put a whole bowl in front of her . . .

unless you want it in your lap or splattered all over the kitchen. Instead, put some finger foods (see opposite) on the tray for her to pick up on her own. Put the bowl on your plate, and feed her while she's attempting to feed herself.

Have four spoons at the ready . . .

two for him and two for you! When they first eat solid food, toddlers bite down on the spoon and grab it. Give him the first spoon. Then use the second one for the second mouthful. Before you know it, he'll be banging the first one and grabbing the second. That's where spoons three and four come in handy. It's kind of like a conveyor belt, replacing one spoon after the other as he grabs each one.

Try to make much of her meal into finger foods

It will not only free you up, it will make her feel more like a 'big girl' who's feeding herself. Don't be surprised when most of what she eats goes on the floor. Prevention is worth a pound of cure. Invest in a large bib with a pocket that catches food. Put a plastic sheet under her seat or high chair. Believe me, if you don't react to her messiness, which is all part of her exploring this new world of solid food, she will probably grow out of the finger-painting-with-her-food stage faster than if you keep trying to stop her or keep her clean.

Don't play food games and don't associate food with play

Everything you do sets an example for your child. If you give him a toy to amuse himself during meals, he'll think mealtime is synonymous with playtime.

Encourage her efforts and praise her appropriately when she exhibits good manners, but when she doesn't, don't take it personally

Remember that your child wasn't born with table manners; she's learning. Of course, you should teach her to say 'please' and 'thank you', but don't become a school mistress. She will learn mealtime etiquette mostly by imitation.

Time for a Sippy Cup? Think H.E.L.P.

- Hold back until she wants a sip from your glass, cup or water bottle.

- Encourage him to experience drinking on his own, but know that until he masters the skill of controlling the flow, all the liquid will come out of the sides of his mouth.

- Limit the mess by putting on a vinyl bib or covering her in a plastic sheet. Limit your own frustration by remembering that she needs practice. (Some parents feed toddlers in their nappies, but I don't recommend it. Civilised people eat in clothes, and as we'll see, what we teach at home, toddlers expect to do elsewhere.)

- Praise only when he manages to actually drink the liquid. Don't say 'good job' when he merely holds the cup up and everything comes spilling out.

Let him get up when he's finished

If you make him sit there and keep presenting bites of food, I assure you he will soon kick, try to wiggle out of the chair or cry. Don't let it get that far.

The Food

As I pointed out earlier, this is your child's domain. Here are other points to keep in mind.

Wean as a preventive measure. Advice today suggests that you wean your baby at six months. Rather than watch the calendar, I suggest that you watch your child and start solid foods sooner rather than later. First of all, if you wait too long, your child may become so accustomed to downing liquids he will reject solids; getting him accustomed to chewing will be a much more troublesome process.

Also, weaning can help prevent sleep disturbances. Granted, sleep disturbances caused by increased mobility and newfound fears are common and unavoidable during the toddler years. However, sleep disruptions caused by a lack of calories can be prevented. If you notice that your child is eating more often during the day, take that as your cue. Instead of nursing him more often or giving him an extra bottle before bed, provide the additional calories he needs in the form of solid food.

Make Your Own

There are lots of high-quality baby foods to be bought, but if you want to make your own, steam or boil fresh vegetables and fruit, and use a food processor or blender to purée them. Freeze in ice-cube trays, which will give you handy one-ounce portions, and the next day transfer the cubes to a plastic bag and defrost as needed. Never add salt to a toddler's diet.

The Whole Milk and Nothing but the Whole Milk!

Between a year and 18 months, whether your child has been on formula or breast milk, introduce whole milk. Toddlers should have at least 24 ounces a day for vitamins, iron and calcium. Start with one bottle a day for the first three days, two bottles for the next three and finally three bottles a day. Cheese, yoghurt and ice cream can substitute for whole milk. Common allergic reactions include excess mucus, diarrhoea, dark circles under the eyes. If your child is allergic or if you want to give soya milk, talk to a nutritionist or your GP.

Remember that weaning is a gradual process

On pages 72–73, I offer 'From Liquids to Solids: A Six-week Starter Plan,' which is a sample weaning routine, beginning at the age of six months. It is meant only as a suggestion. Keep a food log, noting the date and amount of every new food you introduce. It will help both you and your paediatrician in case problems occur.

Introduce finger foods early

Purées are fine, but as your child begins to expand her diet and demonstrates that she can tolerate various foods, give her the same fare in a more adult form – foods she can eat on her own that require a bit more work than mushy substances. Even without teeth, a child as young as seven months can 'gum' certain foods and safely swallow them. Or give her bite-sized pieces that literally melt in her mouth.

Cut finger foods into tiny bits, 1¼-inch square or slightly larger for very soft foods. With vegetables, such as carrots, broccoli or cauliflower, as well as crunchy fruits, like pears and apples, you need to parboil them first.

The What and When of Weaning

Some parents in this country (and some books as well) are confused by the term *weaning*. They think it means to take baby off the breast. In actuality, weaning is the transition from a liquid diet to solid foods. Your baby is probably ready to wean when:

- **She is six months old.** Though babies of previous generations were weaned as young as six weeks, The Food Standards Agency recommends beginning the process from six months. By then, your baby can sit up and control her head; her tongue protrusion reflex has disappeared; her intestines can digest more complex solid foods; and allergies are less likely.

- **He seems hungrier during the day, nurses more or has an extra bottle, and/or wakes up in the middle of the night and takes a full feed.** This suggests that he needs solid foods because he's not getting sufficient calories from breast milk or formula.

- **She shows an interest in food that you're eating.** She might watch you intensely and then, with an open mouth or a reaching gesture, ask for a taste. Or if you're chewing, she might try to poke her finger into your mouth. (In other cultures, mums chew foods and then give it to their babies.)

From Liquids to Solids: A Six-week Starter Plan

Week/Age	7am	9am	11am	1pm	4pm	8pm	Comments
Week 1 26 weeks (6 months)	Baby wakes, feed breast or bottle	4 teaspoons of pears; finish on breast or bottle	Breast or bottle	Breast or bottle	Breast or bottle	Breast or bottle	Start by introducing only one food in the morning; pears are easy to digest
Week 2 27 weeks	Breast or bottle	4 teaspoons of sweet potatoes (or any new food); finish on breast or bottle	Breast or bottle	4 teaspoons of pears; finish on breast or bottle	Breast or bottle	Breast or bottle	Pears move to lunch meal; new food introduced in morning
Week 3 28 weeks	Breast or bottle	4 teaspoons of butternut squash (or any new food); finish on breast or bottle	Breast or bottle	4 teaspoons of sweet potatoes; finish on breast or bottle	4 teaspoons of pears	Breast or bottle	Former new food moves to lunch, now solids are given three times a day
Week 4 29 weeks	Breast or bottle	¼ banana (or any new food); finish on breast or bottle	Breast or bottle	4 teaspoons of sweet potatoes, 4 teaspoons of butternut squash; finish on breast or bottle	4 teaspoons of pears; finish on breast or bottle	Breast or bottle	Quantity increased at midday meal

Week/Age	7am	9am	11am	1pm	4pm	8pm	Comments
Week 5 30 weeks (7 months)	Breast or bottle	4 teaspoons of puréed apples; finish on breast or bottle	Breast or bottle	4 teaspoons of sweet potatoes, 4 teaspoons of pears; finish on breast or bottle	4 teaspoons of butternut squash, ¼ banana; finish on breast or bottle	Breast or bottle	Quantities increased at lunch *and* dinner
Week 6 31 weeks	Breast or bottle	4 teaspoons of green beans, 4 teaspoons of pears; finish on breast or bottle	Breast or bottle	4 teaspoons of butternut squash, 4 teaspoons of apples; finish on breast or bottle	4 teaspoons of sweet potatoes, ¼ banana; finish on breast or bottle	Breast or bottle	As new foods are added, two are given at each meal; quantities also increase, depending on child's appetite

Food Introduction Record

6 Months	7 Months	8 Months	9 Months	10 Months	11 Months	One Year
Apples	Peaches	Brown rice	Avocado	Prunes	Kiwi fruit	Wheat
Pears	Plums	Bagels	Asparagus	Broccoli	Potatoes	Cantaloupe
Bananas	Carrots	Bread	Courgette	Beets	Parsnips	Honeydew
Acorn squash	Peas	Chicken	Yoghurt	Egg-free pasta	Spinach	Oranges
Butternut squash	Green beans	Turkey	Ricotta cheese	Lamb	Lima beans	Watermelon
Sweet potatoes	Barley		Cottage cheese	Mild cheeses	Aubergine	Blueberries
Rice			Cream cheese		Egg yolks	Raspberries
Oats			Beef broth		Pink grapefruit	Strawberries
						Corn
						Tomatoes
						Onions
						Cucumber
						Cauliflower
						Lentils
						Chickpeas
						Tofu
						Fish
						Pork
						Veal
						Egg whites

Make appetising but easy-to-prepare foods for your toddler
If you have a child who likes only two or three different items,
use them to smother other food. Say apple purée is a favourite
– try it on her broccoli.

Can My Child Be a Vegan?
Parents who are vegetarians themselves often ask if it's okay
to put their baby or toddler on a vegetarian diet. Especially
when dairy products and eggs are eliminated, most
vegetarian diets fall short of the minimum daily require-
ments. Also, vegetables are high in bulk but may not give
your child enough vitamin B, calories from fat, or contain
enough iron, which children need for growth. To be on the
safe side, check with your paediatrician or health care
specialist; you may want to contact a nutritionist as well.

Let your child eat in any order and in any combination
Who says apple purée comes after chicken, or that you can't dip
fish into yoghurt? Children learn the rules of eating by sitting at
the table, and they'll eventually imitate them. But in the
beginning, let your child eat the way she wants.

Nutritious snacks are food, too
Before you worry about your child not eating enough, consider
what he eats between meals. Some children can't down a big

meal in one sitting; they do better at 'grazing' throughout the day. That's fine, especially if you give your child healthful snacks, like slightly cooked vegetables or fruits, cheesy crackers, or bite-sized pieces of toast with melted cheese on top.

Early on, allow your child to be part of food preparation

When your child reaches the 'me do' stage, you can't beat 'em, so it's best to join 'em. Children as young as 15 months can help mix, rip lettuce into pieces, decorate cookies, prepare snacks. What's more, cooking develops fine motor skills and, most important, encourages your child's relationship to food.

Avoid labelling any foods as 'bad'

If you demonise certain foods, he will pick up on it and want it more.

Never bribe a child or cajole her with the food

Too often, a parent whose child is about to touch something off-limits or become cranky tries to stave off a meltdown with, 'Here, have a cookie.' Not only is that parent rewarding the behaviour, but the adult is also setting up the child to see food as barter, not a pleasurable commodity. Every human has a lifelong relationship with food. By paying attention to how and when we offer our children food, we will foster their love of eating and their appreciation of good tastes and allow them to enjoy the social interplay as well.

Sample Menu

This is just a guide; it's not God's law. I have a one-year-old in mind here, but what your child eats depends on her weight, temperament and stomach capacity.

Breakfast
¼–½ cup cereal
¼–½ cup fruit
110–180 ml/4–6 ounces either breast or formula milk

Morning Snack
50–110 ml/2–4 ounces fruit juice
Cooked vegetable or cheese

Lunch
¼–½ cup cottage cheese
¼–½ cup yellow or orange vegetable
110–180 ml/4–6 ounces breast or formula milk

Afternoon Snack
50–110 ml/2–4 ounces juice
4 crackers with cheese

Dinner
¼ cup poultry or meat
¼–½ cup green vegetable
¼ cup noodles, pasta, rice or potatoes
¼ cup fruit
110–180 ml/4–6 ounces breast or formula milk

Before Bed
110–180 ml/4–8 ounces breast or formula milk

Food Allergies

It is estimated that 5–6 per cent of babies and young children under the age of three have food allergies. Likely culprits include citrus, egg whites, lamb, berries, some cheeses, cow's milk, wheat, nuts, soya products, carrots, corn, fish and shellfish. This doesn't mean that you don't present any of these foods; just be aware of potential reactions. Allergies are often inherited, but sometimes crop up even when there is no family history. Some studies indicate that 20 per cent or more children grow out of food sensitivities, but it's not because their parents de-sensitise them by giving them more of whatever food they react to. In fact, the opposite often happens: the food allergy becomes more dangerous, and rather than growing out of it, the child has a lifelong problem.

By introducing only one new food per week, if any sign of allergy appears, you'll know what caused it. If your child seems to be sensitive to a new food, stop serving it immediately and don't reintroduce it for at least one month. If he still shows a reaction, wait at least a year and consult a doctor.

Adverse reactions to food are quite serious, the worst being anaphylactic shock, an allergic reaction that affects several organs simultaneously and can be fatal. Milder symptoms usually appear first and might become worse in time:

- Loose stools or diarrhoea
- Rashes
- Puffiness or swelling in the face
- Sneezing, runny nose or other cold-like symptoms
- Wind pains or other symptoms of stomach ache
- Vomiting
- Itchy, watery eyes

Until your child is one year old, just in case he's allergic, avoid egg whites, wheat, citrus (other than pink grapefruit) and tomatoes. After your child is a year old, you can add shredded chicken, scrambled or hard-boiled eggs and soft berries to the list of finger foods, but until at least 18 months, continue to be careful about nuts, which are hard to digest and easy to choke on, as well as shellfish, chocolate and honey.

Dressing for Success

The days of no-hassle dressing are usually over once a child learns how much fun it is to be in motion. Lying on a changing table just doesn't do it for most toddlers. Some will have out-and-out meltdowns over the prospect. Here are some ways I've seen parents head off potential problems.

Get everything ready first
Preparation is key. You don't want to waste time fumbling with these things while your toddler is squirming. Take off the top of the nappy cream, lay out the nappy and have the wipes close by.

Pick the right time
Your child shouldn't be too hungry, too tired, or too involved in play. If he's just about to complete something he's working on and you swoop down and whisk him away, he's not going to be very happy.

Many parents allow toddlers to play in their pyjamas after breakfast, but calling them in later to get dressed can be confusing, especially if a child is involved in play. She hears, 'It's time to get dressed,' but in her mind, she already is! I recommend including 'getting dressed' as the end of your breakfast ritual. The child finishes the meal, brushes her teeth and changes from pyjamas into play clothes in order to get ready for her day.

Announce what you're doing
As you know, I don't believe in ambushing children or taking them by surprise. Let your child know what's happening. 'It's time to get dressed now,' or 'I'm going to change your nappy now.'

Don't rush the process
As much as you may want it 'over with', being in a hurry won't make dressing any easier or faster. With Touchy, Grumpy and Spirited toddlers, in fact, you're really asking for trouble if you rush.

Make dressing fun

Buy loose clothes with elasticised waists, big buttons and Velcro closures. Shirts that can be buttoned or zipped are easier, too. If you buy T-shirts, make sure the opening for the head has buttons at the side, or is big enough or stretchy enough to slip on and off easily.

Talk to your child when you're changing his nappy or dressing him. Continue to explain what you're doing. One good way to amuse and explain is to sing: 'This is the way we put on our shirt, put on our shirt, put on our shirt. This is the way we put on our shirt, so we can go out playing.' If he starts crying, you might try to distract him with what I call a 'no-no toy' – an item that you give him as a treat only when you're changing or dressing him. Excitedly proclaim, 'Ooh, look at what Mum's got!' (I know I always admonish parents to 'start as they mean to go on', but this is one exception. Though you allow your toddler to examine your heirloom watch while changing his nappy, he won't later consider it one of his playthings. Children seem to know that no-no toys are just for the changing table. Besides, changing his nappy and dressing difficulties are usually a short-lived stage.)

Let the child participate

Praise and encourage her effort: 'Good for you, Big Girl. Now you can help Mummy get you undressed.'

Consider alternatives if the prospect of being on the changing table elicits a strong negative reaction

Nappies can just as easily be changed on floors or couches. I've also seen parents try to change a nappy while the child is standing, but I'm not a big fan of that. It's harder to get a secure fit, and your child is more likely to run off before you've finished.

> Don't change your toddler in public. Just because he can't talk yet doesn't mean he considers dressing a spectator sport. After all, would you like to change your clothes in the supermarket, in a park or at the beach in full view of other people? I think not – and neither would your child. If you can't duck into a bathroom or changing room, go to your car. If you have no other option, at least use a blanket or jacket to cover him.

Break up the tasks into smaller pieces

It will take up more of your time and force you to start getting ready earlier. But particularly with reluctant dressers, if you rush you'll have a battle on your hands several times a day. Believe me, by honouring his needs, your child will get through this stage of difficulty faster than if you fight him every step of the way.

Give your child a say in the matter

Although dressing isn't optional, you can offer limited choice as to when, where and what. Needless to say, if you've been chasing your child around the house for an hour, or if she's having a tantrum, such a rational approach won't work. It's best that you take to heart my next point.

Remember that you know best

Whatever diversions you employ to make your child more cooperative, whatever tricks you use to make the process easier, the bottom line is that your child doesn't really have an option when it comes to changing his nappy and getting dressed.

Have an ending ritual

Even if you simply say, 'All dressed!' or 'Now we're ready to go to the park,' this lets the child know that the ordeal is over. He sees the cause and effect: I stayed with it, I'm dressed and now I can play.

Encourage your child to participate in the care of her clothing

Install hooks for pyjamas, bathrobes, jackets and other often-worn items so that she can retrieve and put away certain clothing on her own. Children love to throw dirty clothes in the laundry basket, too. Such care rituals teach your child that some clothes are put away for another day while others go into the wash.

Potty 101

Physical readiness for toilet training depends partially on your child's sphincter muscles. Mums out there know what body part I'm talking about, especially if they had to do Kegel exercises after childbirth. For you dads, next time you go to the loo, try to stop your pee in midstream – your sphincter muscles help you do it. It was once believed that these muscles didn't mature until the age of two, but research is now divided on the subject. In any case, training is both a matter of physical readiness *and* practice. With handicapped children who had no control, we were able to train them by gauging the right times to put them on the toilet. In that case, guidance combined with practice overrides immaturity.

Dressing is a skill that your child will continue to perfect. What I've done above is given you some tools to help him get started. You'll need to be patient and to take your cues from him. When he struggles, help him. But when he says, 'Me do,' let him. Even if you happen to be in a rush one morning, if he has learned to put on even a few items all by himself, you can't expect him to go backwards. Unless you want to do battle with him, don't try to take over. Instead, be a bit late this time and learn that next time you'll have to plan your schedule differently. As I repeatedly point out, toddlers can't tell time, and they certainly don't care if you're late. They care only about their independence.

Giving up Nappies

Getting rid of nappies is the final boundary your toddler will cross as he makes his way across the great divide that separates babies from children. For most children, the optimal time to begin is between 18 months and two years. That said, however, I urge you to look at your child. Let the acronym H.E.L.P. be your guide.

H – Hold back until you see signs that your child is ready

Some children stop dead in their tracks. They stand very still, seem to focus and then suddenly move on.

E – Encourage your child to connect bodily function with words and actions
Once you see that your child's awareness is developing, expand her vocabulary. Whenever you change her nappy, make a point of telling her straight away, 'Oh, this is really wet. It's full of pee.' Now is the time to introduce the actions as well. Invest in a freestanding unit or a potty seat (see sidebar) and start by having her doll or favourite stuffed animal go to the bathroom.

L – Limit your child's time on the potty
No more than two to three minutes at first. This is not about getting your child to perform – it's about teaching him.

P – Praise
Praise your child wildly when she actually deposits something in the toilet bowl – not when she just sits there.

> **Have a Seat, Sonny!**
> I prefer the type of potty seat that goes on top of yours, rather than freestanding units that one has to empty. The former are easier to carry if you're travelling, too. But with both, be careful. Children can easily slip through or get wedged in, either of which can be a scary experience to a child who already has fears of being swallowed up by the bowl! Use a small step stool as a footrest; your child will feel anchored if his feet aren't dangling.

Training Tricks

Here are two creative suggestions from mums whose children are now adults:

- One, the mother of four, didn't use a training seat. Instead, she put her children on the toilet seat backwards. 'That way, they could see what came out of them, and it fascinated them. I had trouble keeping them off the toilet. With each kid, training took no time.'
- The other made training fun by floating Cheerios in the toilet bowl and encouraging her son to have 'target practice'.

The Four Essential Ps of Potty Success

(Pardon the pun, but I just couldn't resist.)

Potty – one that fits his size.

Patience – never rush the process or look disappointed when he doesn't pee or poop; all children progress at their own speed.

Practice – your child needs as much as he can get.

Presence – sit with him and cheer him on.

If you take the initial plunge (sorry – another bad pun) slowly, you'll get to know your child's habits, and your child will more likely be open to the experience. Remember too that your child's personality plays a big role in how receptive he is. Some children are gluttons for the reward of seeing their mother or father go bananas and rejoice in their toilet success; others couldn't care less.

Potty-training Apparel

What does the well-dressed baby-in-training wear? Here are a few points to remember:

- *Nappies.* Disposable nappies are so absorbent nowadays that children don't always recognise when they're wet. Although terry nappies are more work, in the long run they may not be because your child can recognise when she's soiled or wet and may get out of nappies earlier.

- *Training pants.* Like disposable nappies, training pants are very absorbent. As soon as your child starts to recognise where he goes to the potty and the sensation that goes with it, and is able to hold it in until he gets there, he is well on his way. You may want to skip the training-pants stage altogether.

- *Big girl/boy underwear.* When she is going on the potty at least three times a day, try out some 'big girl' (or 'big boy') underwear during the day. If she has an accident, don't make a big deal of it. And never scold! Just change her, wash her bottom and put on a fresh pair of undies.

CHAPTER FIVE
Talking

Language development, like your child's increasing physical prowess, is a slow and steady process.

What Is T.L.C.?

Children of all ages need 'tender loving care', but I have another meaning in mind that will help you guide your child through the critical years of language development. The letters serve as a reminder of the key elements of communication: Talk, Listen, Clarify.

Talk about everything and anything. Describe your day, his activities, things in the immediate environment.

When Will My Child Talk?
The rate of children's language development is determined by various factors. As we discussed in Chapter One, nature and nurture work together. Some factors include:

- Exposure to language and interaction with talkers (constant conversation and eye contact encourage children to talk)

- Gender (girls seem to develop language skills earlier than boys)

- Other developmental gains taking precedence (communication skills may lag when a child starts to walk or expand her social repertoire)

- Birth order (younger children may talk later)

- Genetic disposition (if you or your partner were late talkers, your child might be, too)

Note: sometimes children who start to talk also have setbacks if there is a sudden change in the household – new nanny, new baby, parent goes back to work.

Listen attentively to both your child's verbal and non-verbal expressions so that she feels heard and also learns how to be attentive herself.

Clarify by repeating the correct word or expanding on ideas and without scolding or making your child feel that his speech is 'wrong'.

Hold a running conversation from the moment your child awakens. You can't talk too much to your child (except when she's trying to calm down or fall asleep). It's what young children need; it's how they learn.

Everyday Dialogue

Below are some highlights of a day I spent engaged in conversation with a toddler. The trick is to break down into short sentences what you do each moment of the day.

Morning

Good morning, Viola, my sweet flower! Did you have a good sleep? I missed you. Okay, let's get up. Ooh, you need your nappy changed. You're wet. Can you say 'wet'? That's right: wet. Let's change you and make you clean and comfy. Would you like to hold the cream while Tracy changes you? Okay. All done! Let's go and say hi to Daddy. Say, 'Hi, Daddy.' Okay, now we can go and eat our breakfast. I'll put you in your chair. Up we go! Let's get your bib. What should we have? Do you want banana or apple? Tracy's making your cereal. This is your spoon. Mmmm . . . isn't it good? All done. Let's fill the dishwasher. Do you want to help? Yes? Okay . . . then you put this in. That's right – in it goes.

Errands

We need more food. We have to go shopping. Let's go for a ride. We'll get your shoes. Let me get your coat on. Here we are in the car. Can you say 'car'? Car. Good for you! We're driving to the store. Let me lift you into the trolley. Ooh, look at all the vegetables. Do you see the yellow bananas? Can you say 'banana'? Banana. Good. Here are some green beans. Let's put them into our trolley. Okay, all done. We have lots of food now. Let's go to the checkout. Tracy has to pay the nice lady. Do you want to say hi to her? Thank you. Bye-bye! Look at all our bags. We have to put them in the car. Bye-bye, store!

Playing

Come on, now, let's play. Where's your toy box? Oh, you want to play with your doll? Can you say 'doll'? Doll. Good job! What shall we do with the dolly? Shall we put her in the pram? Should we cover her? Let's put a blanket on her to keep her warm. Uh-oh, dolly is crying. Pick her up and hug her. Is dolly

Parentese Spoken Here

A type of verbal expression that researchers call 'Motherese' or 'Parentese' has been proven very beneficial to the development of young children's language skills. Scientists suggest that Parentese may be nature's way of helping children learn how to talk, because caretakers of all sorts – mothers, fathers, grand-parents, even older siblings – tend to automatically lapse into it when they're around young children because it gets their attention. Anyone who speaks Parentese:

- Is playful and animated
- Looks directly into the child's eyes
- Speaks slowly and in a singsong style
- Enunciates clearly
- Emphasises one word in a sentence
- Repeats words frequently

all better? Oh, dolly is hungry? What shall we give her? Does dolly want a bottle? Can you say 'bottle'? Yes, bottle. Look, dolly is getting tired. Do you want to put her to bed? Let's put her back into the toy box to sleep. Good night, dolly. Can you say 'good night'?

Bedtime

Let's get ready for bed. First, choose a book. Oh, you want this one? Good choice. Can you say 'book'? That's right: book. Good job. Come and sit on my knee. Let's turn the pages. The name of this book is *Brown Bear*. Can you find the brown bear? Well done. Can you say 'bear'? Let's turn the page. Can you find the bluebird? Good, that's the bluebird. All finished now. Let's put the book away. Night-night, book. Say 'night-night'. I'm going to lay you down. But first give Tracy a hug. Mmm, I love you. Here's your blankie.

Night-night, God bless. If you need me, just call. See you in the morning.

T.L.C. Tips: Some Important Reminders

Do . . .

Pay attention to non-verbal as well as verbal signals.

Look your child in the eye when you talk or listen.

Talk in short, simple sentences.

Encourage your child to express himself by asking simple, direct questions.

Play word games in which you and your child interact.

Exercise restraint and patience.

Don't . . .

Talk too loudly, too softly, too quickly, or too anything for that matter.

Shame your child for not pronouncing words correctly.

Phone – Attention = Interruption

It drives me crazy (and I have no doubt other adults feel this way, too) to be on the phone with a friend who is simultaneously admonishing her toddler, 'Now, Benjamin, don't climb up there.' Toddlers (and older kids, too) are opportunists when they don't have your attention, and phone calls, in particular, seem to send a signal: *Mmmm . . . Mum's on the phone – I need her.* My daughter's favourite mischief was getting into the coal scuttle whenever the phone rang.

The truth is most phone calls can wait until your child is napping or in bed. If the phone rings, don't be afraid to say, 'Johnny's up. It's not a good time to talk.' If it's absolutely urgent, at least prepare your child by telling him, 'Mummy has to talk on the phone now.' Give him a favourite toy or activity to keep him busy. Keep the call short and you just might make it through without interruption.

Talk on the phone when your child is talking to you.
Busy yourself with household matters at designated 'child times'.
Interrupt your child.
Use the TV as a baby-sitter.

React appropriately when your child expresses an emotion. When a parent thinks a toddler's 'pout face' is cute and therefore responds by laughing or hugging her because she looks so adorable, that's confusing to the child. Even worse, soon you won't know whether she's pouting to express unhappiness or to get your attention.

Sometimes children go through an echolalia stage – incessant copying of whatever they hear. Instead of answering a question such as, 'Do you want Cheerios or Cocoa Puffs?' they repeat, 'Cheerios or Cocoa Puffs.' Although I certainly believe in encouraging children to speak, in this case a better approach would be to simply ask your child to point to the one he wants.

'No!' is not necessarily a sign that your toddler is obstinate. In fact, he might not even know what it means. Young children often say 'no' because it's a word they hear so often. Therefore, one way to cut down on this seeming negativity is to watch your own cascade of nos. Another is to make sure you talk and listen to your child and give him the attention he needs.

If you've taught your toddler to say, 'Excuse me,' when she interrupts a conversation, when she does it don't tell her, 'Wait a minute until I finish.' First of all, she doesn't know what 'a minute' means. Second, you're sending a mixed message. After all, she followed your rule and then you changed it by asking her to wait. Instead, praise her for being polite and listen to what she has to say. The other adult to whom you're talking will understand.

Clarifying Non-verbal Emotions

You don't have to wait for your child to say words in order to clarify. Your little one sends the following non-verbal cues to tell you how he feels. He'll then look at you for a response. Use his cues and the context to 'read' him and then clarify for him: 'I can see that you're [angry, sad, proud of yourself, happy].'

Cues that mean I'm unhappy, unwilling or angry:
My body is stiff.
I throw my head back.
I throw myself on the floor.
I bang my head.
I bite hard on something, like the sofa.
I cry/scream angrily.

Cues that mean I'm happy and likely to cooperate with you:
I smile and/or laugh.
I coo contentedly.
I clap.
I bounce the top of my body, from the waist up, and jiggle for joy.

What? No Dada?

Much to his father's dismay, a toddler will suddenly start to call everyone, from his uncle to the deliveryman, 'Dad'. Being able to mimic a word doesn't necessarily mean the child understands it. Until he makes that cognitive leap, 'Dada', like many first words, will have a special meaning to that child. But it will take a while for the word to stand for the guy who comes home every night and chases his boy around the living room.

Some fathers have a slightly different complaint. As one recently said to me, 'Alexandra can say "Mama", so why doesn't she say, "Dada", too?' As it turned out, Alexandra hardly ever hears the word 'Dada' because everyone calls her father by his first name. 'And how is your daughter to learn to say *Daddy*,' I asked, 'unless she hears you called it?'

To Talk or Not to Talk

It's important to be aware of red flags (see page 99) that might indicate hearing loss or a developmental delay. But there are also instances in which there is nothing organically wrong with a child, and yet he or she doesn't begin to talk on schedule.

Curling Up with a Good Book (and a Grateful Toddler)

Even babies love to 'read'. Start a child early, and books will become her friends. Don't just read books: change your tone and act out the characters and story. Talk about them, too. The best kind for children under three have:

A simple story line: Younger children like to identify objects, but as they get older, they can follow the sequence of a simple story.

Durability: Especially for children under 15 months, make sure the print is non-toxic and the pages cardboard.

Good illustrations: Bright colours and clear, realistic illustrations are best for young children; as they get older, they can handle fantasy creatures.

Speech Development: What to Look For

I present the chart on page 99 because I know parents like to gauge where their children are. However, there are tremendous developmental variations from child to child; I caution you to use these as broad guidelines only. Remember, too, that many so-called late talkers usually catch up by age three.

Are Two Languages Better than One?

I'm often asked about foreign languages and whether it's a good idea to expose children to more than one. If two languages are spoken in your home, why not? Although sometimes language development is delayed initially, studies indicate that bilingual children are better at cognitive tasks later on. Between ages one and four, children are most receptive to learning more than one language. If they're spoken to in a grammatically correct fashion, they can learn the two simultaneously and will be fluent by age three. So if you and your partner have different native tongues, each should speak in his or her own language. And if you have a nanny who doesn't speak English well, it's better for her to talk in her mother tongue as well.

Age	Speech Milestones	Red Flags
8–12 months	Although some children begin to say 'mama' or 'dada' as young as seven or eight months, by a year most can attach these terms to the right person. They can also respond to one-step commands ('Please, give it to me').	Child does not respond to her name; she doesn't babble either long or short groups of sounds, does not look at people who talk to her, or is not pointing at or making sounds to get what she wants.
12–18 months	As first words, child says simple nouns ('dog', 'baby'), the names of special people and a few action words or phrases ('up', 'go'); may be able to follow one- or two-step commands ('Go to the living room and get your toy').	Child does not say a word or two, even unclearly.
18–24 months	Child may be able to say as many as 10 different words, as well as a great deal of gibberish.	Child does not say more than a few words clearly; by 20 months cannot follow simple request ('Come to Mummy'); does not respond to simple questions with a 'yes' or 'no'.
24–36 months	Child has a word for almost everything; combines words into sentences to express thoughts and feelings; although grammar may be less than perfect, vocabulary is quite extensive; child can carry on actual conversations with adult.	Child uses fewer than 50 words and produces no word combinations; can't under-stand different meanings (up/down) or follow two-step commands; doesn't notice environmental sounds, like a car horn.

CHAPTER SIX
The Real World: Helping Your Child Rehearse Life Skills

Toddlerhood, more than any of life's other passages, is marked by an unprecedented number of firsts, many of which we've already covered – first step, first word, first bite of finger food, first pee in the toilet. Everything about being a toddler is preparation for a more grown-up life. Every new situation and new relationship is a lesson. If we expect young children to cope in the real world, we have to give them the tools to do it and lots of practice as well. That doesn't mean you rush out and enrol your child in swimming lessons. Rather, you start the lessons at home. For each challenge your child will meet, you must plan what I call a rehearsal for change.

A rehearsal is a dry run, a time when actors try out the script and perfect their moves. A rehearsal for change is a way of giving your child practice in the skills she needs to handle various situations in the real world by encouraging her to try them out at home first. Toddlers who can experiment with more adult behaviours in the safe, familiar and controlled arms of the family (eating at a table, sharing, being kind to a pet) tend to have an easier time with unfamiliar experiences outside the house, new people, travel and transitions.

To give your child the practice she needs, see yourself as a director, scheduling and overseeing the various rehearsals. The key to a successful production – her cooperation and willingness to learn – is founded on the bond between the two of you. And if you give her opportunities to practice difficult emotional moments and rehearse *with* you at first, she gets to see that she is competent and can manage herself.

Rehearsals for Change

A relationship or a situation can be a rehearsal for change – a less intimidating, more manageable context that gives your child the practice and skills he needs to handle comparable circumstances in the real world.

• Relationship with you → With other adults → With friends

• Family dinner → Restaurant

• Back garden play → Parks, playgrounds

• Bath and water play at home → Pool, beach

• Having pet at home → Petting and other zoos

• Car rides and quick errands → Shopping

• Short trip and sleep at grandparents' → Long trip and hotel

• Play date → Play group → Toddler class → Preschool

No Matter What the Situation

Successful rehearsals for change . . .

- involve preparation and forethought
- are realistic, taking into consideration what the child can handle
- happen when children are not tired or cranky
- introduce new ideas and skills slowly
- build gradually in duration or intensity
- acknowledge the child's feelings
- show children by adults' example the way they're expected to behave
- end the activity or leave the premises, if possible, before a child gets frustrated or out of control

First Fears: Identifying Emotions and Practising Self-soothing Behaviours

Almost all toddlers have fears of some sort – of separation, of objects or animals, of other adults and children. The best we can do as parents, therefore, is to help our children acknowledge these feelings, let them know it's okay to talk about them and encourage them to learn how to soothe themselves.

Encourage your child to rehearse a full range of emotions

When children don't feel comfortable expressing their feelings they never learn to be in charge of their emotions – to feel them, withstand them and let them pass.

Remember that your child looks to you for guidance, even when you're not consciously giving it

Toddlers can 'catch' fear and anxiety from their elders.

In all situations, at home or on outings, children take their emotional cues from us, which is why parents are so important and influential. Psychologists call this social referencing and have done some fascinating studies to indicate its power. In one, mothers were directed to look into two empty boxes; one red, one green. Looking inside the red one, they said in a monotone, 'Oh.' Looking into the green box, they exclaimed, 'Oh!' in a very upbeat excited voice. Invariably when asked which box he or she would prefer, almost every child chose the green box.

Be there for your child

It is important to be there for your child: if you go into a group and plop your child on the floor and he doesn't like it, I would suggest you get down on the floor with your child at first. If you act like you're there for him, you can get up . . . but do it gradually.

Your style of parenting can also affect your child's willingness to go forth

Heed the power of social referencing and pay attention to the messages you send your child.

Help your child manage her emotions when she doesn't seem able to

One strategy is to give your toddler reality checks about her behaviour; such corrective exchanges at home will serve your child well in the real world.

Applaud her for self-soothing

When your little one feels scared, tired, overwhelmed, abandoned (for that is what it truly feels like to a one-year-old when you say, 'Bye-bye!'), if she naturally turns to an object that signifies comfort or resorts to a behaviour that calms her down, heave a sigh of relief.

> **Rule of Emotional Behaviour**
> To learn how to be in charge of their own emotions and to soothe themselves, children need to experience *all* feelings, even those that *you* may find it hard to witness, like sadness, frustration, disappointment and fear.

First Forays: Practising Public Behaviour

Parents love to take their children on outings. Rehearsals for change increase the odds that these will be pleasant experiences. The trick is to anticipate what will happen in the various settings, analyse what preparation your child will need to handle the situation and then practise the necessary skills at home first.

What's *Your* Security Blanket?

Before you turn your nose up at that smelly old thing your child adores, think about it. Though we adults don't walk around with anything as obvious as a 'binkie' or a stuffed animal, we continue to employ security objects throughout our adult lives. I, for example, always have a tote bag with me containing pictures of my Nan and my children, a few cosmetic items for last-minute freshening up and tampons . . . just in case. When I leave my bag behind, I feel a bit lost. I don't think it's any coincidence that as a toddler my Nan introduced the idea, giving me a little pink bag to tote about that had my favourite toys and keepsakes in it. I'm sure you have your own transitional object, but you may call it a lucky charm, or a practice such as yoga or morning prayer, that makes you more confident to greet the day.

On the Road

Remember that being a travelling parent doesn't make you a Sherpa. It's one thing to include the essentials and to factor in delays and mishaps, but don't feel like you have to line your suitcase with a week's worth of nappies and bring every toy in your toddler's room. There are few places on earth where you can't pick up children's necessities. If your child needs special foods or equipment, and you'll be gone for more than a week, consider shipping such items. You and your toddler will travel more comfortably and less stressfully without unnecessary baggage.

Even if the car ride is only a few hours, try to coincide travel with naptime. Some children get into the habit of conking out a few minutes after departure – and still do it as teenagers! Those who don't nap are likely to get the fidgets. Amuse your child with simple games, like 'Can you see?' (You spot things and say to the child, 'Can you see a doggie? A blue car? An airplane?') Also, prepare a bag of goodies that includes not only favourite items but also a brand-new toy.

> **Rule of Public Behaviour**
> Don't bite off more than your child can chew. If a particular setting proves too much, leave.

First Friendships: Practising Social Behaviour

It's vitally important to include other children in your toddler's life, because early relationships are rehearsals for valuable social skills. Social rehearsals for change involve reinforcing people skills at home and structuring play situations that allow your child to practise them. Here are the pieces that need to come together:

Respect your child's style and pace
The more secure he feels, the more willing he will be to dip his toe into the social stream of life.

Keep your own feelings in check

You may feel embarrassed when your toddler sits on the sidelines: your daughter will sense your disapproval and it will make her feel bad about herself or think that she has done something 'wrong'. It is therefore important to remain patient.

Be persistent

By not allowing the child to go through difficult or scary experiences, you prevent him from practising control and mood management. You inadvertently teach him that it's okay to abandon anything that's hard or uncomfortable. Such children can become butterflies who flit from one thing to another without ever learning to see things through to the end.

Expect replays of social difficulties in new settings

Teaching children to manage their emotions is an ongoing process that requires a great deal of patience. However, it is always better to deal with a child's anxiety or aggression now, to put the time in and let her see that you're there to help her, because she'll have to go through it at some point.

Look at your own social history

Don't let your own past affect the way you direct your child in the present.

Structure situations to meet your child's needs

If you know that your child tends to be reticent, you might want to pick an activity that is less stressful – say, music instead of tumbling. Of course, you might not always have the option.

Prepare your child for the experience

If, for example, you are sending your toddler to day care for the first time then it would be an idea to take him there beforehand. Take your child to the venue once or twice to help get him used to the setting, the staff and the other children – and then only leave him when he is ready.

Arming Your Toddler with Social Skills

Here are the critical skills you'll want to help your child practise, at home and in play situations.

Manners

The best way to teach politeness, of course, is to be polite yourself. So when your child brings you a toy, always say, 'Thank you.' When you want her to cooperate, say, 'Please.'

Empathy

Encourage your child to notice what other children and adults are going through.

Sharing

At around 15 months, children start to grasp the concept of sharing, but they need a lot of help. The goal is to instil in your child a desire to share and to reward that.

A trick I've recommended to mothers, particularly for play dates, is to set a time limit. However, because children don't understand the concept of time, it's best to use a timer. That way, when two children want the same doll, for instance, you can say, 'There's only one doll, so you'll have to take turns. Russell, you go first because you found it. So we'll set a timer. When you hear the buzzer, it's time to give Tina her turn.' Tina is more willing to wait because she knows that when she hears 'Ding!' she gets the doll.

It's important to allow your child to experience disappointment when another child refuses to take turns or share. This, too, is part of life

The Stages of Socialisation: How Your Child Becomes a Social Butterfly

As your toddler matures, his capacity for play naturally grows with him. It helps to understand what each stage looks like from your child's perspective.

Notices other children. Babies as young as two months are fascinated by and curious about other babies and their older siblings. Their eyes will follow them around the room at first. Somewhere around six months, when he's able to reach for objects, your child will reach for other children, too. He wonders what it is, probably thinking it's a kind of mysterious toy. Hey, if I poke this other thing, it cries.

Copies other children. We look at toddlers and think that they're mean, selfish or spiteful when they grab a toy from another child. Actually, your child just wants to copy. Seeing another child use it gives your child ideas, and all of a sudden, a toy that a few moments ago held no interest whatsoever has life to it. Hey, I didn't know that's what that thing does. I want to do it, too.

Plays next to other children. Toddlers don't actually play with each other, they play side by side, which is why it's called 'parallel play'. The idea of sharing and taking turns seems irrelevant to your child, who thinks, Whatever I want to do, I can do, because I'm the only kid in the world.

Plays with other children. By age two and a half or three, most children master basic social skills, and they can mentally imagine things. Therefore, their pretend play is more elaborate, and they can play games that require them to actually cooperate with one another, such as chasing, rolling or kicking a ball back and forth. Now when your child sees a playmate he thinks, 'If I kick this ball to him, he'll kick it back'.

Setting Up Play Dates and Play Groups

Play dates and play groups help children rehearse social skills, but they present quite different challenges. I suggest that you give your toddler both kinds of experience.

A *play date* is usually one-on-one, and it's fairly unstructured. One parent calls another, they set up a time and place (usually, one of their houses or a park) where the two children play together for an hour or two.

Pairing children boils down to common sense. Even though you might like to be with a particular mother, if every week your child ends up being frustrated, having things taken from him, crying – and you start to dread play dates because you're secretly wondering, what's going to happen next week – make play dates with someone else's child and meet your friend for coffee or a game of tennis instead.

If you're hosting a play date, create a safe space where the children can play. Put your pets away. Limit the time – an hour is usually enough before one or the other gets tired. That's when you get conflict.

A *play group* involves two or more children and usually has a more structured format than a play date. The benefit of a play group is that the dynamics are more complex, and it gives children many opportunities to practice the kinds of social skills outlined earlier. However, up to the age of three, I suggest limiting play groups to no more than six children – ideally, four.

If possible, avoid threesomes, which can be difficult because someone usually feels left out.

House rules

A mother I knew drew up a set of house rules for her play group. You may not agree with them, but use them as a guide to create rules of your own.

For the children:
- No eating in the living room.
- No climbing on furniture.
- No aggressive behaviour (hitting, biting, pushing).

For the mothers:
- No older siblings (if one 'crashes', he or she is asked politely to leave).
- Manners should be encouraged.
- If a child is aggressive, he has a time-out until he can behave.
- Broken toys are replaced with new ones.

CHAPTER SEVEN
Teaching Your Child Self-control

The ultimate goal of conscious discipline is to help your child gain self-control. Conscious discipline is about making life predictable for your toddler and setting limits that make her feel secure. It's about your child knowing what to expect and what's expected of her. It's about right and wrong and developing good judgement.

The Twelve Ingredients of Conscious Discipline

Ultimately, conscious discipline empowers our children to learn how to make good choices, be responsible, think for themselves and act in a socially acceptable manner.

1. *Know your own boundaries – and set rules.* Only you can make rules for your household. Think about your boundaries and be consistent.

2. *Look at your own behaviour to see what you're teaching your*

child. The way we handle situations – set limits without anger, act instead of react and deal calmly with stressful situations – is the way we show children how it looks to be in control of our emotions.

3. *Listen to yourself to make sure you are in charge, not your toddler.* Problems occur when parents have no boundaries and let their children set the agenda.

4. *Whenever possible, plan ahead; avoid difficult settings or circumstances.* Limit stimulation and limit situations that are too difficult for your child. Remember that situation can override temperament. Planning may not solve every problem, but it certainly can alleviate the ones that crop up repeatedly . . . as long as we learn from them.

5. *See the situation through your toddler's eyes.* Behaviour that seems 'bad' or 'wrong' to an adult may mean something quite different from a toddler's point of view. Work out what's really going on in each instance. Some misbehaviour is a matter of your toddler being at the wrong place at the wrong time. Or your child may be overtired, a physical state that tends to make toddlers more impulsive and, sometimes, aggressive.

6. *Pick your battles.* Monitoring a toddler can be exhausting. It's important to know when it's absolutely necessary to

enforce your boundaries and when it's okay to relax them a bit. The point is sometimes you need a quick solution. Time is a factor and something has to give. Use your judgement and ingenuity.

7. *Offer closed-end choices.* Toddlers are often more cooperative when offered a choice, because it gives them a sense of control. These have to be real choices, not fake ones. Real choices are alternatives you've narrowed down in your own mind which leave no room for interpretation.

8. *Don't be afraid to say 'no'.* In the long run it is better to say no because life is full of frustration and disappointments, and you need to make sure they are prepared for it.

9. *Nip undesirable behaviour in the bud.* Catch your child before he acts out, or at least in the act. Inappropriate behaviour, whether it's hitting, biting or having a tantrum, must stop regardless of how he feels. The goal is to teach your child to identify and manage his emotions.

10. *Praise good behaviour and correct or ignore bad.* Sadly, some parents are so focused on 'no', they forget to notice when their child does things right.

Offering Choices

Demands/Threats	Choice Statements/Questions
If you don't eat, we're not going to the playground.	When you've finished eating, then we can go to the playground.
Get over here . . . now.	Do you want to come over here by yourself or should I get you?
You have to have your nappy changed.	Do you want me to change your nappy now, or after we read this book?
Let go of Sally's toy.	If you can't let go of Sally's toy, I can help you.
No, Paul – you cannot play with my lipstick.	Do you want to give me that lipstick or should I help you let go of it? Thank you – what good cooperation. Now would you like to hold my comb or my mirror?
Don't slam that door again.	Please close the door gently.
Stop talking with food in your mouth.	Finish chewing and then you can talk to me.
No! We are not going to stop for ice cream on the way home. You'll ruin your appetite.	Yes, I know that you're hungry. You can have a [mention a delicious snack] as soon as we get home.

11. *Don't rely on corporal punishment.* My feeling is that if you hit a child or demonstrate violence in any shape or form, you have lost control and it's you, not your child, who requires help.

12. *Remember that giving in doesn't equal love.* Quite the contrary: if you give in, you are helping your child see that cooperation is fun and that it feels good to behave nicely. When you are consistent and clear about your rules, not only do you feel better about yourself and the kind of parent you are, your child also feels secure. He knows your boundaries and respects you for your word. He loves you for your honesty, knowing that when you say something, you follow through.

When your child is upset, rather than cajoling, which ignores his feelings, or trying to convince him that he doesn't 'really' feel bad, which encourages him to hide his feelings, allow him to fully express all his emotions. Say things like, 'I know you're disappointed,' or 'It looks like you're really angry about that,' to let him know it's normal to have emotional reactions and even to be unhappy.

Be aware of what you 'reward' with your attention – whining, crying, nagging, yelling, running in church. Instead, praise your child when she cooperates and acts kindly, when she's quiet, when she plays independently and when she lies down to soothe herself. In short, make the good moments last by acknowledging them.

Why You Shouldn't Spank

I believe that any type of hitting is bad. When people rationalise ('A little swat here or there never did *me* any harm') or minimise ('It was just a tap'), in my mind it's like someone with a drinking problem saying, 'I only drink beer.'

It's a momentary solution. Spanking doesn't teach a child anything about misbehaviour. It only teaches them that it hurts to get hit. He may behave better for a while, because he naturally wants to avoid pain. But then the child doesn't learn any skills, and he's certainly not developing inner control.

It's unfair. When a big person loses control and hits a little person, he or she is being a bully.

It's a double standard. How can you hit a child when you're angry or frustrated and not expect her to turn around and do the same thing?

It encourages aggression. As my Nan says, 'You bear the devil in,' meaning that you make children *more* defiant by hitting them. Research backs her up: children who are spanked tend to hit peers, especially those who are younger or smaller, and try to solve problems with violence.

Short Fuse Alert!

Even parents who are against spanking can spontaneously strike a child. It sometimes happens out of fear, a knee-jerk reaction when a child runs into the road or courts danger in some other way. Or it's the result of parental frustration. You lose control and hit because your child repeatedly does something annoying

– for example, tugging at your sleeve or pulling on a magazine you're reading. Even if you only deliver a tap on the bottom, take responsibility and apologise. Say, 'I'm sorry. It was wrong for Mummy to hit you.'

Look in the mirror. In what ways are you not taking care of yourself? Are you eating properly, getting enough rest, having marital problems? If so, your fuse could be shorter than usual.

Assess the circumstances. Was there something about this particular situation that hit a personal hot spot? Once you know what your triggers are, try to avoid similar situations or at least remove yourself before your blood starts to boil. We all have our breaking points. Here are the most common answers when parents are asked, 'What sets you off?'

- Noise

- Whining

- Sleeping problems

- Crying, especially inconsolable or excessive crying

- Testing behaviour (you ask the child not to do something and he keeps at it)

Don't feel guilty. Every parent makes mistakes; don't beat yourself up. Laying yourself at your child's feet gives him too much control. Guilt also can make it hard for you to discipline him properly in the future.

Going Too Far

Following are common mistakes parents make when trying to discipline their children that involve saying too much or saying things beyond a young child's grasp:

Overexplaining: A classic real-life example occurs when a toddler is about to climb on to a chair and the parent launches into an elaborate explanation: 'If you climb up there you might fall and hurt yourself.' Instead of talking, the parent should take action and physically restrain the child.

Being vague/obtuse: Certain statements, such as 'No, that's dangerous,' have a number of meanings. Instead, saying 'Don't climb on the steps' is specific and clear. Likewise, statements such as 'Would you like it if I hit you?' (commonly uttered when a child hits) don't mean anything to a toddler either. Better to say, 'Ouch, that hurts. You may not hit.'

Taking it personally: I cringe when a parent says, 'It makes me sad when you misbehave.' Telling children that their behaviour causes you to feel unhappy gives them too much control and power. It also implies that they are responsible for your moods. It's better to say, 'When you behave like that, you can't be around us.'

Pleading/apologising: Discipline has to be delivered without ambivalence and with a sense that you're in control of your emotions. A parent who pleads ('Please don't hit Mummy') and then goes on to apologise ('It makes Mummy sad when she has to give you a time-out') doesn't seem to be in charge.

Not managing your own anger: Discipline should come from a compassionate place inside you, not from anger. Never threaten your child. Moreover, it's best not to hold on to your feelings. Your toddler will quickly forget about it, and so should you.

The Rule of One/Two/Three

Pay attention to the messages that you send your child. Especially in highly impressionable young children, bad habits can develop quickly. To every situation, whether it's whining or a full-blown tantrum, apply this simple One/Two/Three rule:

One. The first time your child does something that crosses a line you've set, you take notice. You also let the child know that she's crossed the line.

Two. The second time it happens, suspect that you're witnessing the onset of a pattern and that the behaviour could become habitual. Hence, if your child hits you again, put her down and remind her of the rule: 'I told you, you can't hit Mummy.' Then remove your child from the room. Don't do it with anger; simply take her out and explain, 'You cannot play with the other children if you hit.' If you're firm to begin with, your child will probably stop.

Three. If a negative behaviour pattern continues, you have to ask yourself, What am I doing to perpetuate it? Some toddlers test constantly; they see how far they can go, what reaction they get, what's responded to. Some lose control more often than others. But through it all, they're looking to their parents to set limits.

Respectful Intervention

- State the rule: 'No you may not . . .'

- Explain the effect of the behaviour: 'That . . . hurts/made Sara cry/isn't nice.'

- Make the child apologise and give the other child a hug: 'Say, I'm sorry.' (But don't let your toddler use 'sorry' to gloss over the bad behaviour.)

- Explain the consequence: 'When you [restate the behaviour], you may not stay; we'll have to leave until you calm down.' (This may also be a good opportunity for a time-out; see page 128)

Know Yourself

Parenting style is strongly linked to attitudes about discipline and to the actions parents take.

The Controller is apt to discipline in anger. She often yells at or yanks her child or, even worse, punishes physically.

The Enabler is likely to apologise for her child, make excuses for her behaviour. She doesn't do much to discipline her child until a situation gets so out of hand she's forced to take action.

The H.E.L.P.er strikes a happy medium. She hangs back long enough to let her child work out difficulties on his own and to evaluate the situation, but intervenes immediately and respectfully when necessary. She knows it's important for her child to have his feelings, so she doesn't try to talk him out of them or cajole him into a good mood. She is able to make rules and levy consequences when her child oversteps the boundaries she's set.

The Tantrum Two-step

Tantrums, unfortunately, go with the territory of early childhood. They are essentially attention-seeking behaviour and

> **Thoughts on Embarrassment**
> Yes, it's embarrassing when your child has a meltdown, but it's not as embarrassing as if he keeps doing it. Therefore, before you try to amuse your child or give him something to appease his anger, consider this: if you don't change the pattern, you're in for countless repeat performances.

loss of control. While you may not be able to escape tantrums altogether, you can discourage your child from using tantrums to subvert your rules or overstep your boundaries. My suggestion is actually a simple two-step process, whereby you analyse (understand what caused the tantrum) and act.

1. *Analyse* Understanding the cause of a particular tantrum gives you clues about how to stop it. Fatigue, confusion, frustration and overstimulation are all common causes.

A lot of temper tantrums also happen because toddlers can't express themselves, and if you observe carefully, you'll see that your child may be trying to tell you something. Worst of all, though, are the 'I-want-what-I-want' tantrums, which are designed to manipulate and control the environment – in other words, you.

One way to tell the difference between tantrums designed to manipulate and those that result from frustration or a physical cause, such as fatigue or overstimulation, is to apply the simple ABC technique:

A stands for the antecedent – what came first. What were you doing at the time? What was your toddler doing?

B stands for the behaviour – what your toddler did. Did she cry? Did she bite, push or hit? Is what she did something that she never does? Often does?

C stands for the consequence – the usual result of A and B. Here it's important to take responsibility for how your actions shape your child. The key to changing the consequence, therefore, is to do something different – allow the child to have his feelings but not try to appease or cave in to his demands.

2. *Act* The best way to stop a tantrum is to remain calm yourself and to allow the child to ride out the emotions without an audience. In other words, take away the attention that the tantrum was meant to elicit. To that end, I prescribe the Three Ds:

Distract. Your toddler's short attention span can be a gift when he's on the verge of a meltdown.

Detach. As long as your child is not endangering herself, someone else, or property, it's best to ignore a full-blown tantrum.

> **Anger Cues: What's Happening to Me?**
>
> Just as important as tuning in to your child's moods is the knowledge of how you change when your child stamps her feet, says 'no', or has an out-and-out melt-down in public. I asked mothers how their bodies tell them they are about to lose it. If you don't recognise yourself in any of the following, figure out what your physical anger cues are.
>
> 'I get hot all over.'
> 'I get hives.'
> 'I start to take it personally.'
> 'My heart beats faster.'
> 'It's almost as if I stop breathing.'
> 'My chest starts heaving, and I breathe faster.'
> 'My palms sweat.'
> 'I start grinding my teeth.'

Disarm. When children have tantrums, they are not in control of their emotions. An adult has to help them calm down. Some respond well to a parent's arms encircling them, while others become even more agitated when restrained. You also can disarm by removing a child from the setting that upset her in the first place.

Use the D that feels most appropriate, or use all three. You need to assess the situation and also gauge what might be most effective with your child. No matter which of the Ds you employ, it's important to check into your own emotional state as well.

When you feel your blood starting to boil, leave the room. Give yourself a time-out.

Time-out!

What It Is: The use of a 'time-out' period is sorely misunderstood. It's not about taking a child to her room as punishment. It's a method of avoiding a full-scale battle, a time away from the heat of the moment. A proper time-out helps a child regain control over her emotions and prevents parents from accidentally reinforcing the bad behaviour. With toddlers, I advise parents to do time-outs *with* their children, not ever to leave them alone in a crib or playpen.

How It's Done: If you're at home, take your child away from the scene of the crime. Say he has a tantrum in the kitchen; bring him into the living room and sit with him until he calms down. If your child acts up in public or at another person's house, take him into another room. In either instance, tell him what you expect of him. 'No, we may not go back until you're quiet.' He understands more than you realise. Verbal reinforcement, accompanied by being taken away from the situation, will get your message across. Return when he's calm and quiet, but if he starts misbehaving, leave again.

What You Say: Name the emotion ('I can see you're angry . . .') and tell him the consequence ('. . . but you may not throw your food'). End with a single, simple sentence: 'When you behave like this you can't be around [us/other children].' Do not say, 'We don't want you around.'

What Not to Do: Never apologise: 'I don't like to do this to you' or 'It makes me feel sad that you're in time-out.' A child should never be yanked or yelled at; rather, calmly lead him away from the centre of the action. Never lock your toddler in a room alone.

Conscious Discipline: A Simple Guide

Challenge	What to Do	What to Say
Overstimulation.	Remove him from the activity.	I can see that you're getting frustrated, so let's take a little walk outside.
Tantrum in public place because he wants something.	Ignore it.	Wow, that's impressive, but you still can't have it.
	If that fails, remove him.	You can't behave like this in [wherever you are].
Refusing to cooperate when dressing.	Stop, wait a few minutes.	When you're ready we'll start again.
He continues to run around.	Stop him; pick him up.	We can leave when you have your shoes and socks on.
Shouting.	Lower your own voice.	Can we use our quiet voice, please?
Whining.	Look her in the eye and imitate a 'best' (non-whining) voice.	I can't listen unless you use your best voice.
Running where it's not appropriate.	Restrain him by putting two hands on his shoulders.	You may not run here. If you continue, we'll have to leave.

Challenge	What to Do	What to Say
Kicking or hitting when you pick her up.	Put her down immediately.	You may not hit/kick me. That hurts.
Grabbing toy from another child.	Stand up, go near child and encourage her to give it back.	William was playing with that. We need to give it back to him.
Throwing food.	Take him down from high chair.	We don't throw food at the table.
Pulling another child's hair.	Put your hand over whichever hand is wrapped around the other child's hair; stroke your child's hand.	Be gentle, no pulling.
Hitting another child.	Restrain him; if he is agitated, take him outside or to another room until he calms down.	You may not hit. That hurts Jim.
Hitting repeatedly.	Go home.	We have to leave now.

The Dummy Habit

The older your child is, the more difficult it will be to break the dummy habit, no matter which method you use. In any case, before you attempt to eliminate the dummy, introduce a comfort item if your child doesn't already have one. Once he becomes attached to a silky or a stuffed animal, he might automatically become less dependent on his dummy.

Gradual Elimination

Start by cutting down during the day. For three days, allow your child to start naps with his dummy, but as soon as he's sleeping, take it out of his mouth. For the next three days, eliminate the dummy at naptime. (I assume you will have already familiarised him with a comfort item.) Simply say, 'No more dummy for naptime.' If he cries, comfort him, rather than sticking an inanimate object into his mouth. Give him his security item, hug him or pat him, making your physical presence known, and say, 'You're okay, honey. You can sleep now.'

Once your little one is accustomed to napping without a dummy – if he's under eight months, it usually takes about a week, longer if he's older – then do the same thing at night. First, allow him to fall asleep with the dummy in his mouth and then take it away. He may wake up in the middle of the night, crying for his dummy, which he's probably been doing all along. The difference now, though, is that you withhold it. Comfort him with gestures, not conversation, and make sure that he has his security object in hand. Don't give in or act like you feel sorry for him. After all, you're doing a good deed here: you're teaching him the skill of going to sleep on his own.

Cold Turkey

I don't recommend cold turkey – sudden withdrawal – for children under a year, because they have trouble understanding what 'all gone' means. However, older children sometimes have no trouble giving up their dummy, especially when they realise it's simply not there for them. As one mum told her little one, 'Oh, dear, dummy's gone.'

'Where'd it go?' her daughter asked.

'Dust bin,' said Mum cheerily.

Now, that little one probably didn't even know what a dust bin was, but she accepted her dummy's demise and went on with her life. Some children will cry for an hour, but then seem to forget about it. Others will keep asking and continue to be upset, but this rarely lasts for more than a few days. Twenty-two-month-old Ricky, for instance, went absolutely nuts when his dad told him one day, 'Your dummy is gone. It was making your teeth bad.' Ricky couldn't have cared less about his teeth. He cried and cried, but Dad, to his credit, didn't show any emotion in response to his son's tears. He didn't say, 'Oh, poor Ricky. His dummy's gone.' Three nights later, Ricky got over it.

A Combined Approach

Some parents do a combination of gradual elimination and cold turkey. To break 11-month-old Ian of his dummy habit, Marissa made his relinquishing it part of their wake-up ritual. Every morning, she'd greet him, give him a big hug, extend her hand and say, 'Now it's time to give Mummy your dummy.' Without a fuss, Ian would turn over his dummy. For the next month, though, he continued to sleep with his dummy. Observing him at night, Marissa realised that Ian's dummy was not a habit that disturbed his sleep, because he didn't wake up once it slipped out of his mouth. So one night Marissa finally sprang it on him: 'No more dummy. You're a big boy.' And that was that.

Whatever method you use, be realistic. After all, this is a kind of 'withdrawal' experience for your child, but hang in there. Expect a few nights of crying. Eventually, it will get better. And in years to come, the getting-rid-of-the-dummy story will work its way into your family folklore.

CHAPTER EIGHT

When Baby Makes Four: Growing Your Family

Asking the parents of a toddler, 'When are you going to have another one?' or 'Are you trying yet?' is enough to make their brave souls tremble. In this chapter, we'll look at the issue of future children, how to prepare and help your toddler deal with a sibling and, just as important, how to keep yourself and your relationship on an even keel.

Small Children/Great Expectations

It's one thing to deal with your own issues, but quite another to handle a toddler who may not be old enough to understand why your belly is swelling or why you can no longer whisk her up into your arms. Here are some stop-gap measures that can make the transition a little smoother.

Remember that your child doesn't get it
Your child might proudly point to your bulging belly and parrot the right words, but he has no idea what the new arrival will mean to him.

Don't tell too soon
However, you know your child, so base your decision on his personality. Obviously, if your child notices that your waistline is expanding, and asks about it, make that your starting point.

Six months before the baby is due, get your toddler into a play group
Sharing and cooperation are lessons best taught with peers. Being with other children will at least give her some undertanding of what it's like to share.

Display affection for other children
Let your toddler observe you interacting with other little ones.

Expose your toddler to babies
Read him books about baby brothers and sisters. Also make him aware of how fragile babies are.

Many expectant parents customarily take hospital tours and bring their toddler along, thinking that it will give them a sense of where Mummy will go to have the baby. I disagree. Hospitals can be a scary place for a young child. It can also be confusing to think that 'the baby' is going to come from the place where people go when they're sick.

Be sensitive to your toddler's point of view
Even though she doesn't fully understand what's happening on an intellectual level, I can assure you that your child knows things are changing. Be conscious of your words and, most important, don't tell her how much she's going to love her new sibling, because she might not!

Plan to stay out overnight without your toddler
This way he will have had some overnight experience without you; remind him of the fun he had and that, just like last time, you'll see him soon.

Use your common sense and trust your instinct
Don't take everything you hear as gospel.

Wean your toddler, if possible
You need to figure out ways of reassuring and comforting her without the use of your breast. It's also a good idea to introduce a security object now, before the baby is born, and to help her find ways to self-sooth.

Feelings Alert!
Statements like these aren't 'cute'. They tell you how your child feels, so pay attention when you hear:

- I don't like it when she cries.
- She's ugly.
- I hate her.
- When is the baby going back?

Enter the Intruder

You can't blame any toddler for feeling displaced when a new baby joins the family. The following bits of advice might help minimise this momentous transition.

Schedule one-on-one time with your toddler

When the baby first comes and sleeps a lot, steal little bits of time to be with your firstborn. Allow your older child to help in small ways, but don't ask him to be too grown up.

Accept, but don't encourage, regressive behaviour

If your child goes through a period of regression, don't overreact. It's quite common. Encourage your child to express how she feels.

Note: A baby can be a sitting (or lying) duck for an older sibling, even one who seems to love and accept her. Never leave your toddler and the baby alone. Even if you're in the room with them, you need eyes in the back of your head.

Watch what you say

Toddlers imitate whatever they hear and see around them. Your child is always listening, and it's easy to plant ideas in his head.

Never use the baby as an excuse, as in, 'We have to leave now because it's Jonathan's naptime.'

Try to 'catch' your child being kind and loving to his sibling and praise him: 'What a good brother you are,' or 'That's so sweet of you to hold Gina's hand.'

Take your older child's complaints seriously

When your child complains, look at her history: is this something she was used to and now feels deprived of? Consider the nature of her request, too. If what she wants is reasonable – and it doesn't hurt or exclude the baby – then accommodate her.

Let your child know what you expect

If you're busy with the baby, say so. Your child has to get used to hearing it. When she is mean or harms the baby, tell her. Anticipate 'testing' – but be firm about your boundaries.

Things You Should Never Say to Your Toddler about His Younger Sibling

'You have to take care of him.'
'You have to like her.'
'Be nice to the new baby.'
'You have to protect our baby.'
'Don't you love your new baby?' Then when the toddler says, 'No,' you say, 'Oh, yes you do.'
'Play with your sister.'
'Look after your little brother.'
'Watch your sister while I'm cooking dinner.'
'Share with your brother.'
'You're a big boy now.'
'Act your age.'

Nip It in the Bud
When your toddler feels neglected, he is not able to say, 'By the way, Mummy, I need your attention for the next half hour.' He becomes angry and impulsive instead. And he knows that hurting the baby will get your attention. So whenever your little one decides to have a go at the new baby, do what you would in the situations we described earlier. Restrain his hand, and without anger, say, 'You may not stay here if you pinch the baby. That hurts her.' The lesson here is that it's not okay to act out your feelings by bullying another human being or animal.

Try to not overreact

When your toddler pulls an impish stunt to get your attention, it can frustrate the Dickens out of you – and your instinct is to blow your top. However, overreacting only reinforces bad behaviour.

Don't allow 'the baby' to break the rules either

Don't constantly ask the older child to share or make excuses when the baby invades, or destroys, his playthings. Hearing 'Oh, he's just a baby – he doesn't know what he's doing,' will frustrate the older child even more. Because your toddler doesn't have the maturity to make allowances for that annoying little creature with grubby hands, his first instinct might be to retaliate physically.

Set up a special place for your older one

You can't really baby-proof your house with a three-year-old because they love little things, so I would suggest making a place that is exclusively for her.

Treat each child as an individual

It's often easier to keep the peace when each child is dealt with fairly and individually. Even though you love both children, you can't possibly feel the same about them – they are different.

Have a long-term outlook

When you're tired of being a juggler and referee, remember that your children won't be a baby and a toddler for ever.

The Benefits of Siblinghood

The next time your toddler pinches the baby, or the baby knocks down the older one's LEGO castle, remind yourself that research reveals good news about siblings, too.

- *Language.* Even when your older child is making goo-goo eyes at the baby, he's teaching him to converse. Often a child's first words are the direct result of these lessons.

When the Older Child Has a Tantrum

A mother's worst nightmare is being alone with a young baby and a screaming toddler. In fact, your toddler usually chooses times when you're involved with the baby to act up. What better time to have a meltdown? They know you're captive – and you are. Someone has to wait, and it can't be the baby.

As I instructed Elaine, 'The next time Nanette has a tantrum when you're busy with Ethel, finish what you're doing with the baby, put her into her cot, and give Nanette a time-out.' I also pointed out that aside from wanting to keep the baby safe, the reason you deal with her first is to send a message to the older child that tantrums don't get your attention.

- *Intelligence.* Obviously, younger siblings imitate and thereby learn from their elders. But it works the other way as well: children's intellect grows whenever they help another child solve a problem, even one who is younger. Siblings also spur each other on to explore and be creative.

- *Self-esteem.* Helping a brother or sister and having someone who praises you and loves you unconditionally boosts confidence.

- *Social skills.* Siblings watch and model one another. From their elder brother or sister the younger one will learn the rules of social interaction, figure out how to behave in various situations, how to get a parent to say 'yes'.

- *Emotional sustenance.* Siblings can help one another travel the rocky terrain of life. An older sibling can help a younger one prepare for new experiences and show her the ropes; a younger sibling can cheer an older one on. Having a sister or brother also gives children practice in airing feelings and developing trust.

Avoiding Chore Wars

- Be fair.
- Make reasonable compromises.
- Whenever possible, each partner should be allowed to do what he or she likes best and/or is best at doing.
- Make time for each other.
- Get a baby-sitter or ask Grandma or a good friend to pitch in.

Couple Conflicts

The bigger a family gets, the more complex its dynamics and when parents don't work as a team or when unresolved issues fester, it can also cause a child's behaviour to spin out of control.

Problem Prevention

- Air resentments instead of letting them fester – but don't argue about them in front of your toddler.

- Attempt to solve problems together; make a plan for dealing with sleep, meals, outings. At times you may have to agree to disagree.

- Toddlers do best with consistent standards, but they can handle differences, as long as you're up-front about them: You can have three books with Dad, but when Mummy puts you to bed she reads two books.

- Try not to polarise your positions by going to one extreme because you think your partner is at the other.

- Listen to what you say to your child. When Dad says, 'Mummy doesn't like it when you put your feet on the couch,' it tells your child you disagree and subtly undermines Mum's standards.

- Don't take your child's reactions personally – children behave differently with each parent.

- If fighting becomes chronic, seek professional help.

Time for You/Time for Your Relationships

One of the best ways to guard against couple conflicts, of course, is to replenish your own energy and to protect your adult relationships – not just your marriage but your friendships as well.

- Make specific plans for adult time.
- When you take a break, really take a break.
- Find ways to take brief respites.
- Exercise.
- Pamper yourself.
- Keep the sparks glowing.
- Create a parent support system.
- Enlarge your definition of 'family'.
- Don't forget to ask for help.

Self-care is the key to juggling. Otherwise we start to feel like it's all too much. We fight with our partners, yell at our children. Resentment builds and frustration mounts. Parenting is hard and ever changing. It's not an admission of failure to ask for help – it's the sign of a wise parent.

Epilogue

Some Final Thoughts

Being a good parent is both gratifying and self-affirming, but it's also a hard job, harder still with a toddler underfoot. Every day ushers in breathtaking change, and the stakes seem higher than in the good old days when a feed or a nappy change was often all that was needed to make your child happy. Now the issues are more complex. Is he walking okay? Talking enough? Will he have friends? Will people like him? Will he be scared on his first day of preschool? And how can I make it all happen... *now*?

This book has been about what you can do to help your toddler negotiate this daunting life passage. But I end it by stressing as well what you *cannot* do. You can encourage and nurture, but you can't push. You can step in to avert or solve problems, but you cannot rescue. You can, and should, be in charge, but you cannot control who your child is. No matter how eager you are to have him reach the next developmental plateau or get past a difficult phase, he will walk, talk, make friends, and develop in ways that even you can't imagine... on his time, not yours.

You must have patience. Cheer your child on, love her unconditionally, help her prepare for life, and give her all the tools she'll need to carry on without you. And when she's ready, the world and everything in it will be waiting for her.

Index

☐ Secrets of the Baby Whisperer	9780091857028	£10.99
☐ Tops Tips from the Baby Whisperer	9780091917449	£6.99
☐ Secrets of the Baby Whisperer for Toddlers	9780091884598	£10.99
☐ The Baby Whisperer Solves All Your Problems	9780091902513	£10.99

FREE POST AND PACKING
Overseas customers allow £2.00 per paperback.

ORDER:

By phone: 01624 677237

By post: Random House Books
c/o Bookpost
PO Box 29
Douglas
Isle of Man, IM99 1BQ

By fax: 01624 670923

By email: bookshop@enterprise.net

Cheques (payable to Bookpost) and credit cards accepted

Prices and availability subject to change without notice.
Allow 28 days for delivery.
When placing your order, please mention if you do not wish to receive
any additional information.

www.rbooks.co.uk